Lesbian, Gay, Bisexual. and Transgend Issues in Social W

A Comprehensive Bibliography with Annotations

▼

Compiled by

James I. Martin, Ph.D.
Ehrenkranz School of Social Work
New York University

Ski Hunter, Ph.D.
School of Social Work
University of Texas at Arlington

Council on Social Work Education
Alexandria, Virginia

Council on Social Work Education
1725 Duke Street, Suite 500
Alexandria, VA 22314-3457

Printed in the United States of America

Lesbian, Gay, Bisexual, and Transgender Issues in Social Work: A Comprehensive Bibliography with Annotations

Compiled by James I. Martin and Ski Hunter

ISBN 0-87293-083-1

Contents

Introduction

For those of us who have researched, taught about, practiced with, or advocated on behalf of lesbian, gay, bisexual, transgender, and two-spirit (lgbtt) populations for more than a few years, the recent explosion of literature relevant to these activities is truly exciting. Gone are the days in which there were few written materials about these populations for inclusion in social work curricula, to support students and faculty in scholarship efforts, or to help inform practitioners about their needs and experiences. Practitioners and academics in social work and related fields are publishing such materials at an increasing rate. They include, but are certainly not limited to, practitioners and academics who are themselves lesbian, gay, bisexual, transgender, or two-spirit. We believe the commitment of CSWE toward achieving full participation of these members of the profession contributes to this trend, as do CSWE mandates for inclusion of lesbian and gay content throughout the social work curriculum.

We hope that this bibliography will be a contribution toward the fulfillment of two of the responsibilities of the CSWE Commission on Sexual Orientation and Gender Expression, which we co-chair. The Commission is responsible for advancing the development and availability of curriculum resources on the experiences of lgbtt persons, and issues that are relevant to them. Advocating for full participation of lgbtt persons in CSWE and social work education is another of the Commission's responsibilities. We hope that by adding to the interest and knowledge about these populations in social work education and practice in general, this bibliography might help to support those faculty, administrators, students, and practitioners who are themselves lgbtt, as well as those advocating on their behalf.

This bibliography is a compendium of references to recently-published books, book chapters, and journal articles running the full gamut of the social work curriculum. It includes brief annotations for some references in each category. All of the entries have relevance to social work education and practice in that they either address issues with which social work education or practice concerns itself or they address interventions that are used in social work.

In compiling this bibliography, we gave careful attention to social work authors and to publications either in social work journals or with specific references to social work. However, we also included relevant works both by non-social work authors and published in non-social work journals. Because of the tremendous growth of this literature in recent years, we had to limit ourselves to works published only during the last few years. With very few exceptions, this bibliography is limited to works published between 1993 and August, 2000. In addition, space did not allow us to include publications in languages other than English or those focusing on lgbtt persons or social work practice in countries other than the United States. Even with these exclusions, space did not allow us to include every book, chapter, and article published since 1993 on relevant topics or annotations for all of the materials we did include. In some instances in which multiple works addressed the same or similar topics, we did not include all of them. Its limitations notwithstanding, this bibliography represents what we believe to be a comprehensive guide to the most recent and best literature available on lgbtt persons and lgbtt issues related to social work.

Compiling this bibliography has allowed us to see both the strengths and the weaknesses of the literature in these areas. There is a great need for more research and writing about transgender persons and their experiences, and about gender transgression in general. While more literature is available on bisexuals and bisexuality, it too is limited at the present time. Although there is increasing attention to the complexities of lesbian, gay, bisexual, and transgender identities, there remains a great deal to be learned about the ways in which sexual orientation interacts with gender and its expression, and with race, ethnicity, social class, culture, age, disability, and other variables. We know too little about the implications of these interactions for people's identities, life experiences, and needs for social work intervention. There also remains a great need for more literature on interventions with lgbtt clients in all modalities, especially those combining a detailed explanation of the intervention model or underlying theory with extensive case examples. Finally, there is little known about the effectiveness of any interventions with these populations.

We wish to thank CSWE for the opportunity to create and disseminate this bibliography. We thank in particular Michael Monti, director of publications and media, who suggested the project and then made it easy for us to accomplish. We are also indebted to Yuet Lam Tong for her cheerful diligence and for the considerable time she devoted to obtaining from NYU Bobst Library many of the articles and books that we reviewed for inclusion in this bibliography.

James I. Martin
Ski Hunter

I. Overview

Books on Multiple Topics

1. Appleby, G. A., & Anastas, J. W. (1998). *Not just a passing phase: Social work with gay, lesbian, and bisexual people.* New York: Columbia University Press.

    In addition to examining gay, lesbian, and bisexual people's experiences across the lifespan, this book describes the development and complexity of their identities, culture, and communities. It includes special sections on mental health and substance abuse, HIV/AIDS, and violence.

2. Bohan, J. S. (1996). *Psychology and sexual orientation: Coming to terms.* New York: Routledge.

3. Bullough, B., Bullough, V. L., & Elias, J. (Eds.). (1997). *Gender blending.* Amherst, NY: Prometheus.

4. Denny, D. (Ed.). (1998). *Current concepts of transgendered identity.* New York: Garland.

    This book presents historical data on transgender persons, sexual reassignment, and research and treatment issues.

5. Firestein, B. A. (Ed.). (1996). *Bisexuality: The psychology and politics of an invisible minority.* Thousand Oaks, CA: Sage Publications.

    This edited book presents topics on bisexuality such as managing multiple identities, AIDS, and politics and community.

6. Greene, B. (Ed.). (1997). *Ethnic and cultural diversity among lesbians and gay men.* Thousand Oaks, CA: Sage Publications.

7. Greene, B., & Croom, G. L. (1999). *Education, research, and practice in the lesbian, gay and transgendered psychology: A resource manual.* Thousand Oaks, CA: Sage Publications.

8. Haeberle, E. J., & Gindorf, R. (Eds.). (1998). *Bisexualities: The ideology and practice of sexual contact with both men and women.* New York: Continuum.

9. Hunter, S., Shannon, C., Knox, J., & Martin, J. I. (1998). *Lesbian, gay, and bisexual youths and adults: Knowledge for human services practice.* Thousand Oaks, CA: Sage Publications.

    This book covers a number of topics such as community development, heterosexism, coming out, parenting, and the life course.

10. Laird, J., & Green, R. J. (Eds.). (1996). *Lesbians and gays in couples and families: A handbook for therapists.* San Francisco: Jossey-Bass.

11. Mallon, G. P. (Ed.). (1998). *Foundations of social work practice with lesbian and gay persons.* New York: Harrington Park Press.

    This book presents an overview of direct practice at all levels of intervention with lesbians and gay men. It includes a chapter on applying social work values and ethics in work with these populations, and another on the conflicting allegiances often experienced by lesbians and gay men of color.

12.   Mallon, G. P. (Ed.). (1999). *Social services with transgendered youth.* New York: Harrington Park Press.

13.   Perez, R. M., DeBord, K. A., & Bieschke, K. L. (2000). *Handbook of counseling and psychotherapy with lesbian, gay, and bisexual clients.* Washington, DC: American Psychological Association.

14.   Van Wormer, K., Wells, J., & Boes, M. (2000). *Social work with lesbians, gays, and bisexuals: A strengths perspective.* Needham Heights, MA: Allyn & Bacon.

15.   Weinberg, M. S., Williams, C. J., & Pryor, D. W. (1994). *Dual attraction: Understanding bisexuality.* New York: Oxford University Press.

Resources On Sexual Orientation & Gender Expression

16.   Bailey, J. M. (1995). Biological perspectives on sexual orientation. In A. R. D'Augelli & C. J. Patterson (Eds.), *Lesbian, gay, and bisexual identities over the lifespan: Psychological perspectives* (pp. 102-135). New York: Oxford University Press.

This chapter examines several possible meanings of construing sexual orientation as biologically determined, and it exhaustively reviews the empirical evidence for theories about the biological determination of sexual orientation.

17.   Broido, E. M. (2000). Constructing identity: The nature and meaning of lesbian, gay, and bisexual identities. In R. M. Perez & K. A. DeBord (Eds.), *Handbook of counseling and psychotherapy with lesbian, gay, and bisexual clients* (pp. 13-33). Washington, DC: American Psychological Association.

18.   Bhugra, D., & De Silva, P. (1998). Dimensions of bisexuality: An exploratory study using focus groups of male and female bisexuals. *Sexual and Marital Therapy, 13,* 145-157.

19.   Cole, S. S., Denny, D., Eyler, A. E., & Samons, S. L. (2000). Issues of transgender. In L. T. Szuchman & F. Muscarella (Eds.), *Psychological perspectives on human sexuality* (pp. 149-195). New York: John Wiley & Sons.

20.   Corbett, K. (1998). Cross-gendered identifications and homosexual boyhood: Toward a more complex theory of gender. *American Journal of Orthopsychiatry, 68,* 352-360.

21.   Ellis, A. L., & Mitchell, R. W. (2000). Sexual orientation. In L. T. Szuchman & F. Muscarella (Eds.), *Psychological perspectives on human sexuality* (pp. 196-231). New York: John Wiley & Sons.

This chapter summarizes theory and research on sexual orientation. It examines the relationship of sexual orientation with sexual identity and the relationship of these variables with mental health.

22.   Feinberg, L. (1996). *Transgender warriors.* Boston: Beacon Press.

This book describes the author's development of an identity as a transgender person, and examines gender boundary transgression across history. It includes a portrait gallery and brief biographies of several transgender persons, and an International Bill of Gender Rights.

23. Fox, R. C. (1996). Bisexuality: An examination of theory and research. In R. P. Cabaj & T. S. Stein (Eds.), *Textbook of homosexuality and mental health* (pp. 147-171). Washington, DC: American Psychiatric Press.

    This chapter reviews bisexuality in psychoanalytic theory, lesbian and gay identity theory, sexual orientation theory, sexuality research, and theory and research that focused on bisexuality and bisexual identities.

24. Gagné, P., & Tewksbury, J. R. (1999). Knowledge and power, body and self: An analysis of knowledge systems and the transgendered self. *Sociological Quarterly, 40,* 59-83.

25. Kitzinger, C. (1995). Social constructionism: Implications for lesbian and gay psychology. In A. R. D'Augelli & C. J. Patterson (Eds.), *Lesbian, gay, and bisexual identities over the lifespan: Psychological perspectives* (pp. 136-161). New York: Oxford University Press.

26. Paul, J. P. (1996). Bisexuality: Exploring/exploding the boundaries. In R. C. Savin-Williams & K. M. Cohen (Eds.), *The lives of lesbians, gay men, and bisexuals: Children to adults* (pp. 436-461). Fort Worth, TX: Harcourt Brace.

27. Rust, P. C. (1995). *Bisexuality and the challenge to lesbian politics: Sex, loyalty, and revolution.* New York: New York University.

28. Weber, J. C. (1996). Social class as a correlate of gender identity among lesbian women. *Sex Roles, 35,* 271-280.

Descriptions of Populations

29. Bodlund, O., & Kullgren, G. (1996). Transsexualism—General outcome and prognostic factors: A five-year follow-up study of nineteen transsexuals in the process of changing sex. *Archives of Sexual Behavior, 25,* 303-316.

30. Boykin, K. (1996). *One more river to cross: Black & gay in America.* New York: Anchor Books.

    This book describes what it is like to be Black and gay in the United States. It examines the similarities and differences in the oppression experienced by Black people and gay and lesbian people, and it describes how racism and homophobia present challenges to those who are Black and gay and who attempt to integrate these two identities.

31. Brown, L. B. (Ed.). (1997). *Two spirit people: American Indian lesbian women and gay men.* New York: Harrington Park Press.

32. Brown, M. S., & Rounsley, C. A. (1996). *True selves: Understanding transsexualism—For families, friends, coworkers, and helping professionals.* San Francisco: Jossey-Bass.

33. Chauncey, G. (1994). *Gay New York: Gender, urban culture, and the making of the gay male world, 1890-1940.* New York: Basic Books.

    This book describes in great detail how gay male identities evolved in New York City during the first half of the twentieth century. The analysis depicts differing identity constructions according to social class, race, and ethnicity. It clarifies the relationship between sexual orientation and gender expression among gay men.

34. Faderman, L. (1991). *Odd girls and twilight lovers: A history of lesbian life in twentieth-century America.* New York: Penguin Books.

    This book describes how love between women evolved to contemporary lesbian identities in the United States during the twentieth century. It examines a variety of subcultures constructed within the context of social class, age, race, and ethnicity.

35. Gagné, P., & Tewksbury, J. R. (1998). Conformity pressures and gender resistance among transgendered individuals. *Social Problems, 45,* 81-101.

    This article reports data from 65 male-to-female transgender persons about the pressure to conform to and to resist binary enactments of gender.

36. Saewyc, E. M., Skay, C. L., Bearinger, L. H., Blum, R. W., & Resnick, M. D. (1998). Demographics of sexual orientation among American-Indian adolescents. *American Journal of Orthopsychiatry, 68,* 590-600.

37. Tewksbury, R., & Gagne, P. (1996). Transgenderists: Products of non-normative intersections of sex, gender, and sexuality. *Journal of Men's Studies, 5*(2), 105-129.

38. Udis-Kessler, A. (1996). Challenging the stereotypes. In S. Rose & C. Stevens (Eds.), *Bisexual horizons: Politics, histories, lives* (pp. 45-57). London: Lawrence & Wisehart.

39. Williams, M. J. (1999). *Sexual pathways: Adapting to dual sexual attraction.* Westport, CT: Praeger.

Sexuality

40. Blasius, M. (1994). *Gay and lesbian politics: Sexuality and the emergence of a new ethic.* Philadelphia: Temple University Press.

41. Brown, L. S. (2000). Dangerousness, impotence, silence, and invisibility: Heterosexism in the construction of women's sexuality. In C. B. Travis & J. W. White (Eds.), *Sexuality, society, and feminism* (pp. 273-297). Washington, DC: American Psychological Association.

42. Coleman, E., & Rosser, B. R. (1996). Gay and bisexual male sexuality. In R. P. Cabaj & T. S. Stein (Eds.), *Textbook of homosexuality and mental health* (pp. 707-721). Washington, DC: American Psychiatric Press.

    This chapter examines the sexuality of men who are gay or bisexual. It includes information about sexual behavior among gay couples and some problems that gay and bisexual men might experience in their sexual functioning.

43. Deenen, A. A., Gijs, L., & Van Naerssen, A. X. (1994). Intimacy and sexuality in gay male couples. *Archives of Sexual Behavior, 23,* 421-431.

44. Fausto-Sterling, A. (2000). *Sexing the body: Gender politics and the construction of sexuality.* New York: Basic Books.

45. Hall, J. (1999). An exploration of the sexual and relationship experiences of lesbian survivors of childhood sexual abuse. *Sexual and Marital Therapy, 14,* 61-70.

46. Herbert, S. E. (1996). Lesbian sexuality. In R. P. Cabaj & T. S. Stein (Eds.), *Textbook of homosexuality and mental health* (pp. 723-742). Washington, DC: American Psychiatric Press.

This chapter examines the sexuality and sexual behavior of lesbian and bisexual women. It also describes problems that lesbians may experience in their sexual functioning, and gives guidelines for assessing and managing these problems clinically.

47. Pope, M. (1997). Sexual issues for older lesbians and gays. *Topics in Geriatric Rehabilitation, 12,* 53-60.

48. Warner, M. (1999). *The trouble with normal: Sex, politics, and the ethics of queer life.* New York: Free Press.

    This book describes the relationship between sexual shame, stigma, and sociopolitical moralism among contemporary gay men and lesbians. It criticizes the contemporary gay and lesbian movement for its abandonment of sexual liberationist values.

Community & Culture

49. Atkins, D., & Marston, C. (1999). Creating accessible queer community: Intersections and fractures with Dis/Ability Praxis. *Journal of Gay, Lesbian, and Bisexual Identity, 4,* 3-21.

50. Burstein, H. E. (1999). Looking out, looking in: Anti-semitism and racism in lesbian communities. *Journal of Homosexuality, 36,* 142-157.

51. D'Augelli, A. R., & Garnets, L. D. (1995). Lesbian, gay, and bisexual communities. In A. R. D'Augelli & C. J. Patterson (Eds.), *Lesbian, gay, and bisexual identities over the lifespan* (pp. 293-320). New York: Oxford University Press.

52. Esterberg, K. G. (1994). From accommodation to liberation: A social movement analysis of lesbians in the homophile movement. *Gender & Society, 8,* 424-443.

    This article focuses on the Daughters of Bilitis, a homophile organization founded in 1956 for women.

53. Esterberg, K. G. (1996). Gay cultures, gay communities: The social organization of lesbians, gay men, and bisexuals. In R. C. Savin-Williams & K. M. Cohen (Eds.), *The lives of lesbians, gay men, and bisexuals: Children to adults* (pp. 377-391). Fort Worth, TX: Harcourt Brace.

54. Irvine, J. M. (1994). A place in the rainbow: Theorizing about lesbian and gay culture. *Sociological Theory, 12,* 232-248.

    This article examines the controversy about gay and lesbian persons as a culture, definitions of culture, and who should claim the cultural status.

55. Lord, K. B., & Reid, C. A. (1995). Drawing lines in the dirt: Rural lesbian communities— Models of self-definition and self-determination. *Journal of Gay & Lesbian Social Services, 3,* 13-21.

56. McCarthy, L. (2000). Poppies in a wheat field: Exploring the lives of rural lesbians. *Journal of Homosexuality, 39,* 75-94.

57. Valentine, G. (1994). Toward a geography of the lesbian community. *Women & Environments, 14*(1), 8-10.

    This article discusses differences between lesbian communities and gay communities.

II. Anti-GLBT Oppression

Heterosexism & Homophobia

1. Baker, J. G., & Fishbein, H. D. (1998). The development of prejudice towards gays and lesbians by adolescents. *Journal of Heterosexuality, 36*(1), 89-100.

2. Clarke, V. (2000). Stereotype, attack and stigmatize those who disagree: Employing scientific rhetoric in debates about lesbian and gay parenting. *Feminism & Psychology, 10,* 152-159.

3. Corley, T. J., & Pollack, R. H. (1996). Do changes in the stereotypic depiction of a lesbian couple affect heterosexuals' attitudes toward lesbianism? *Journal of Homosexuality, 32*(2), 1-17.

4. Eliason, M. J. (1997). The prevalence and nature of biphobia in heterosexual undergraduate students. *Archives of Sexual Behavior, 26,* 317-326.

5. Fisher, R. D., Derison, D., Polley, C. F., Cadman, J., & Johnston, D. (1994). Religiousness, religious orientation, and attitudes towards gays and lesbians. *Journal of Applied Social Psychology, 24,* 614-630.

6. Friend, R. A. (1998). Undoing heterosexism and homophobia: Moving from "talking the talk" to "walking the talk." *Journal of Sex Education and Therapy, 23,* 94-104.

    This article identifies five factors needed for systematic dismantling of heterosexism in schools and organizations: shared leadership, inclusive policies, practices, and pedagogy, resources, a plan, and ongoing and inclusive communication.

7. Herek, G. M. (1995). Psychological heterosexism in the United States. In A. R. D'Augelli & C. J. Patterson (Eds.), *Lesbian, gay, and bisexual identities over the lifespan: Psychological perspectives* (pp. 321-346). New York: Oxford University Press.

8. Herek, G. M. (Ed.). (1998). *Stigma and sexual orientation: Understanding prejudice against lesbians, gay men, and bisexuals.* Thousand Oaks, CA: Sage Publications.

    This book discusses antigay prejudice, stereotypes, and behaviors against LBG persons in various contexts and the consequences of these phenomena for the well-being of LGB persons.

9. Herek, G. M. (2000). The psychology of sexual prejudice. *Current Directions in Psychological Science, 9*(1), 19-22.

    This article defines and discusses sexual prejudice, its prevalence, psychological correlates, underlying motivations, and relation to hate crimes and other antigay actions.

10. Herek, G. M., & Capitanio, J. P. (1995). Black heterosexuals' attitudes toward lesbians and gay men in the United States. *The Journal of Sex Research, 32,* 95-105.

11. Herek, G. M., & Capitanio, J. P. (1996). "Some of my best friends": Intergroup contact, concealable stigma, and heterosexuals' attitudes toward gay men and lesbians. *Society for Personality and Social Psychology, 22,* 412-424.

12. Herek, G. M., & Capitanio, J. P. (1999). Sex differences in how heterosexuals think about lesbians and gay men: Evidence from survey context effects. *The Journal of Sex Research, 36,* 1-26.

13. Johnson, M. E., Brems, C., & Alford-Keating, P. (1997). Personality correlates of homophobia. *Journal of Homosexuality, 34*(1), 57-69.

14. LaMar, L., & Kite, M. (1998). Sex differences in attitudes toward gay men and lesbians: A multidimensional perspective. *The Journal of Sex Research, 35,* 189-196.

15. Livingston, J. A. (1996). Individual action and political strategies: Creating a future free from heterosexism. In E. D. Rothblum & L. A. Bond (Eds.), *Preventing heterosexism and homophobia* (pp. 253-265). Thousand Oaks, CA: Sage Publications.

16. Logan, C. R. (1996). Homophobia? No, Homoprejudice. *Journal of Homosexuality, 31*(3), 31-51.

    This article discusses findings that suggest that anti-"homosexual" responses do not result from a phobia but primarily from prejudice.

17. Martinez, D. G. (1998). Mujer, latina, lesbian—notes on the multidimensionality of economic and sociopolitical injustice. *Journal of Gay & Lesbian Social Services, 8*(3), 99-112.

    This article addresses the impact of economic and sociopolitical injustice on Latina lesbians along four dimensions: anti-gay violence and sexual harassment/victimization, employment discrimination, marginalization by the white lesbian and gay community, and heterosexism within traditional Hispanic communities.

18. Mohr, J. J., & Rochlen, A. B. (1999). Measuring attitudes regarding bisexuality in lesbian, gay male, and heterosexual populations. *Journal of Counseling Psychology, 46,* 353-369.

19. O'Hare, T., Williams, C., & Ezoviski, A. (1996). Fear of AIDS and homophobia: Implications for direct practice and advocacy. *Social Work, 41,* 51-58.

    This article reports on a survey of the relationship between homophobia and fear of AIDS among social workers with attitudes concerning rights for gay and lesbian persons.

20. Romo-Carmona, M. (1995). Lesbian latinas: Organizational efforts to end oppression. *Journal of Gay & Lesbian Social Services, 3*(2), 85-93.

21. Schwanberg, S. L. (1996). Health care professionals' attitudes toward lesbian women and gay men. *Journal of Homosexuality, 31*(3), 71-83.

22. Simoni, J. M. (1996). Pathways to prejudice: Predicting students' heterosexist attitudes with demographics, self-esteem, and contact with lesbians and gay men. *Journal of College Student Development, 37,* 68-78.

23. Waldo, C. R. (1999). Working in a majority context: A structural model of heterosexism as minority stress in the workplace. *Journal of Counseling Psychology, 46,* 218-232.

24. Wong, F. Y., McCreary, D. R., Carpenter, K. M., Engle, A., & Korchynsky, R. (1999). Gender-related factors influencing perceptions of homosexuality. *Journal of Homosexuality, 37*(3), 19-31.

Acts of Violence & Harassment

25. Biaggio, M. (1997). Sexual harassment of lesbians in the workplace. *Journal of Lesbian Studies, 1*, 89-106.

26. Cogan, J. C. (1996). The prevention of anti-lesbian/gay hate crimes through social change and empowerment. In E. D. Rothblum & L. A. Bond (Eds.), *Preventing heterosexism and homophobia* (pp. 219-238). Thousand Oaks, CA: Sage Publications.

27. Comstock, G. D. (1991). *Violence against lesbians and gay men.* New York: Columbia University Press.

     This book is a seminal examination of anti-gay and anti-lesbian violence. It reviews the empirical research on victims and perpetrators of such violence, and discusses a variety of ways in which these violent acts might be understood.

28. D'Augelli, A. R. (1998). Developmental implications of victimization of lesbian, gay, and bisexual youths. In G. M. Herek (Ed.), *Stigma and sexual orientation: Understanding prejudice against lesbians, gay men, and bisexuals.* Thousand Oaks, CA: Sage Publications.

29. Franklin, K. (2000). Antigay behaviors among young adults: Prevalence, patterns, and motivators in a noncriminal population. *Journal of Interpersonal Violence, 15*, 339-362.

30. Herek, G. M., & Berrill, K. T. (Eds.). (1992). *Hate crimes: Confronting violence against lesbians and gay men.* Newbury Park, CA: Sage Publications.

     This book includes a collection of papers presented at a workshop on violence against lesbians and gay men that was sponsored by the National Institute on Mental Health. There are theoretical and research-based chapters on the social context of violent acts, incidence trends, the experience of victims and perpetrators, and policy recommendations.

31. Herek, G. M., Gillis, J. R., & Cogan, J. C. (1999). Psychological sequelae of hate-crime victimization among lesbian, gay, and bisexual adults. *Journal of Consulting and Clinical Psychology, 67*, 945-951.

     This article reports on a survey of hate-crime victimization on a large sample of lesbian, gay, and bisexual adults. It describes differences between the psychological effects of hate-crime and non-hate-crime victimization on members of the sample.

32. Herek, G. M., Gillis, J. R., Cogan, J. C., & Glunt, E. K. (1997). Hate crime victimization among lesbian, gay, and bisexual adults: Prevalence, psychological correlates, and methodological issues. *Journal of Interpersonal Violence, 12*, 195-215.

33. Hershberger, S. L., & D'Augelli, A. R. (1995). The impact of victimization on the mental health and suicidality of lesbian, gay, and bisexual youths. *Developmental Psychology, 31,* 65-74.

     This article uses structural equation modeling to test the theory that threats or actual incidents of physical and verbal abuse have direct and indirect effects on the mental health of lesbian, gay, and bisexual youths.

34. Mallon, G. P. (1998). *We don't exactly get the welcome wagon.* New York: Columbia University Press.

35.   Onken, S. (1998). Conceptualizing violence against gay, lesbian, bisexual, intersexual, and transgendered people. *Journal of Gay & Lesbian Social Services, 8*(3), 5-24.

      This article applies a multisystemic model in order to conceptualize the full range of violence experienced by glbt individuals and communities in American society, and to explain how such violence has its origins in oppressive forces operating on multiple levels.

36.   Otis, M. D., & Skinner, W. F. (1996). The prevalence of victimization and its effect on mental well-being among lesbian and gay people *Journal of Homosexuality, 30*(3), 93-121.

37.   Peel, E. (1999). Violence against lesbians and gay men: Decision-making in reporting and not reporting crime. *Feminism & Psychology, 9*, 161-167.

38.   Pilkington, N. W., & D'Augelli, A. R. (1995). Victimization of lesbian, gay, and bisexual youth in community settings. *Journal of Community Psychology, 23*, 34-56.

39.   Savin-Williams, R. C. (1994). Verbal and physical abuse as stressors in the lives of lesbian, gay male, and bisexual youths: Associations with school problems, running away, substance abuse, prostitution, and suicide. *Journal of Consulting and Clinical Psychology, 62*, 261-269.

40.   Savin-Williams, R. C., & Cohen, K. M. (1996). Psychosocial outcomes of verbal and physical abuse among lesbian, gay, and bisexual youths. In R.C. Savin-Williams & K. M. Cohen (Eds.), *The lives of lesbians, gays, and bisexuals: Children to adults* (pp. 181-200). Fort Worth, TX: Harcourt Brace.

41.   Waldo, C. R., Hesson-McInnis, M. S., & D'Augelli, A. R. (1998). Antecedents and consequences of victimization of lesbian, gay, and bisexual young people: A structural model comparing rural university and urban samples. *American Journal of Community Psychology, 26*, 307-334.

III. Life Course Development

Adolescence

1.   Anderson, A. L. (1998). Strengths of gay male youth: An untold story. *Child and Adolescent Social Work Journal, 15*(1), 55-71.

2.   Anhalt, K., & Morris, T. L. (1998). Development and adjustment issues of gay, lesbian, and bisexual adolescents: A review of the empirical literature. *Clinical Child and Family Psychology Review, 1*, 215-230.

      This article reviews the empirical literature on adjustment difficulties of glb adolescents, including suicide attempts, substance use and abuse, conduct issues, and academic issues.

3.   Besner, H. F., & Spungin, C. I. (1995). *Gay and lesbian students: Understanding their needs.* Washington, DC: Taylor & Francis.

4.   D'Augelli, A. R. (1996). Enhancing the development of lesbian, gay, and bisexual youths. In E. D. Rothblum & L. A. Bond (Eds.), *Preventing heterosexism and homophobia* (pp. 124-150). Thousand Oaks, CA: Sage Publications.

5. D'Augelli, A. R. (1996). Lesbian, gay, and bisexual development during adolescence and young adulthood. In R. P. Cabaj & T. S. Stein (Eds.), *Textbook of homosexuality and mental health* (pp. 267-287). Washington, DC: American Psychiatric Press.

    This chapter discusses developmental milestones, major stressors, mental health issues, and identity consolidation.

6. Durby, D. D. (1994). Gay, lesbian, and bisexual youth. *Journal of Gay and Lesbian Social Services, 1*, 1-37.

7. Faulkner, A. H., & Cranston, K. (1998). Correlates of same-sex sexual behavior in a random sample of Massachusetts high school students. *American Journal of Public Health, 88*, 262-266.

8. Floyd, J. F., Stein, T. S., Harter, K. S., Allison, A., & Nye, C. L. (1999). Gay, lesbian and bisexual youths: Separation-individuation, parental attitudes, identity consolidation, and well-being. *Journal of Youth and Adolescence, 28*, 719-739.

9. Garofalo, R., Wolf, R. C., Wissow, L. S., Woods, E. R., & Goodman, E. (1999). Sexual orientation and risk of suicide attempts among a representative sample of youth. *Archives of Pediatric and Adolescent Medicine, 153*, 487-493.

    This chapter discusses the risk for suicide among gay and lesbian adolescents, studies of attempts and completions, and clinical issues.

10. Grossman, A. H. (1997). Growing up with a "spoiled identity": Lesbian, gay and bisexual youth at risk. *Journal of Gay & Lesbian Social Services, 6*(3), 45-55.

    This article discusses how stigma and internalized homophobia put gay and lesbian youth at risk for numerous negative outcomes including chemical use and dropping out of school.

11. Grossman, A. H., & Kerner, M. S. (1998). Support networks of gay male and lesbian youth. *Journal of Gay, Lesbian, and Bisexual Identity, 3*, 27-46.

12. Hershberger, S. L., Pilkington, N. W., & D'Augelli, A. R. (1997). Predictors of suicide attempts among gay, lesbian, and bisexual youth. *Journal of Adolescent Research, 12*, 477-497.

13. James, S. E. (1998). Fulfilling the promise: Community response to the needs of sexual minority youth and families. *American Journal of Orthopsychiatry, 68*, 447-454.

14. Lock, J., & Steiner, H. (1999). Gay, lesbian, and bisexual youth risks for emotional, physical, and social problems: Results from a community-based survey. *Journal of the American Academy of Child and Adolescent Psychiatry, 38*, 297-304.

15. Mallon, G. P. (1999). Gay and lesbian adolescents and their families. *Journal of Gay & Lesbian Social Services, 10*(2), 69-92.

16. Nesmith, A. A., Burton, D. L., & Cosgrove, T. J. (1999). Gay, lesbian, and bisexual youth and young adults: Social support in their own words. *Journal of Homosexuality, 37*(1), 95-108.

17. Owens, R. E. (1998). *Queer kids: The challenges and promise for lesbian, gay, and bisexual youth.* New York: Haworth Press.

18. Proctor, C. D., & Groze, V. K. (1994). Risk factors for suicide among gay, lesbian, and bisexual youths. *Social Work, 39*, 504-513.

19. Radkowsky, M., & Siegel, L. J. (1997). The gay adolescent: Stressors, adaptations, and psychosocial interventions. *Clinical Psychology Review, 17,* 191-216.

> **This article discusses how social stigmatization creates obstacles to achieving the tasks of adolescence and leads to outcomes of loneliness, isolation, depression, and suicide among gay adolescents.**

20. Remafedi, G., French, S., Story, M., Resnick, M. D., & Blum, R. (1998). The relationship between suicide risk and sexual orientation: Results of a population-based study. *American Journal of Public Health, 88,* 57-60.

21. Rosario, M., Meyer-Bahlburg, H. F., Hunter, J., Exner, T. M., Gwadz, M., & Keller, A. M. (1996). The psychosexual development of urban lesbian, gay, and bisexual youths. *Journal of Sex Research, 35,* 113-126.

22. Rotheram-Borus, M. J., Rosario, M., Van Rossem, R., Reid, H., & Gillis, R. (1995). Prevalence, course, and predictors of multiple problem behaviors among gay and bisexual male adolescents. *Developmental Psychology, 31,* 75-85.

> **This article examines multiple problem behaviors, stress, and personal resources among 136 mostly Black and Latino gay and bisexual male adolescents.**

23. Savin-Williams, R. C. (1995). An exploratory study of pubertal maturation timing and self-esteem among gay and bisexual male youths. *Developmental Psychology, 31,* 56-64.

24. Savin-Williams, R. C. (1996). Ethnic- and sexual-minority youth. In R. C. Savin-Williams & K. M. Cohen (Eds.), *The lives of lesbian, gay men, and bisexuals: Children to adults* (pp. 152-165). Fort Worth, TX: Harcourt Brace.

25. Savin-Williams, R. C. (1998). *"...and then I became gay": Young men's stories.* New York: Routledge.

> **This book reports on interviews with gay and bisexual youth about coming out and disclosure, relationships, diversity among gay youth, and other topics.**

Young Adulthood

26. Berg-Cross, L. (1997). Lesbians, family process and individuation. *Journal of College Student Psychotherapy, 3,* 97-112.

> **This article discusses college-age lesbians and how they try to individuate from their family of origin regarding issues such as coming out and their relationships with same-sex lovers.**

27. Eliason, M. J. (1996). A survey of the campus climate for lesbian, gay, and bisexual university members. *Journal of Psychology & Human Sexuality, 8*(4), 39-58.

28. Rhoads, R. A. (1994). *Coming out at college: The struggle for a queer identity.* Westport, CT: Bergin & Garvey.

Midlife Adulthood

29.   Christian, D. V., & Keefe, D. A. (1997). Maturing gay men: A framework for social service: Assessment and intervention. *Journal of Gay & Lesbian Social Services, 6*(1), 47-78.

This article presents a typological model of three sociosexual integrative fields (sexual market, primary relationship, and social network) that help identify some of the problems and hazards of gay male aging.

30.   Cohler, B. J., Hostetler, A. J., & Boxer, A. M. (1998). Generativity, social context, and lived experience: Narratives of gay men in middle adulthood. In D. P. McAdams & E. de St. Aubin (Eds.), *Generativity and adult development* (pp. 265-309). Washington, DC: American Psychological Association.

31.   Isay, R. A. (1998). Heterosexually married homosexual men: Clinical and developmental issues. *American Journal of Orthopsychiatry, 68*, 424-432.

32.   Kertzner, R. (1999). Self-appraisal of life experience and psychological adjustment in midlife gay men. *Journal of Psychology & Human Sexuality, 11*(2), 43-63.

33.   Kertzner, R. M., & Sved, M. (1996). Midlife gay men and lesbians: Adult development and mental health. In R. P. Cabaj & T. S. Stein (Eds.), *Textbook of homosexuality and mental health* (pp. 289-303). Washington, DC: American Psychiatric Press.

34.   Kimmel, D. C., & Sang, B. E. (1995). Lesbians and gay men in midlife. In A. R. D'Augelli & C. J. Patterson (Eds.), *Lesbian, gay, and bisexual identities over the lifespan: Psychological perspectives* (pp. 190-214). New York: Oxford University Press.

35.   Kooden, H. (1997). Successful aging in the middle-aged gay man: A contribution to developmental theory. *Journal of Gay & Lesbian Social Services, 6*(3), 21-43.

36.   Rothblum, E. D., Mintz, B., Cowan, D. B., & Haller, C. (1996). Lesbian baby boomers at midlife. In K. Jay (Ed.), *Dyke life: A celebration of the lesbian experience* (pp. 61-76). New York: Basic Books.

This chapter discusses how the concerns of midlife lesbians differ from those of heterosexual midlife women.

Old Age

37.   Adleman, J. (1996). We never promised you role models. In K. Jay (Ed.), *Dyke life: A celebration of the lesbian experience* (pp. 77-94). New York: Basic Books.

38.   Beeler, J. A., Rawls, T. W., Herdt, G., & Cohler, B. J. (1999). The needs of older lesbians and gay men in Chicago. *Journal of Gay & Lesbian Social Services, 9*(1), 31-49.

39.   Berger, R. M., & Kelly, J. J. (1996). Gay men and lesbians grown older. In R. P. Cabaj & T. S. Stein (Eds.), *Textbook of homosexuality and mental health* (pp. 305-316). Washington, DC: American Psychiatric Press.

40.   Boxer, A. M. (1997). Gay, lesbian, and bisexual aging into the twenty-first century: An overview and introduction. *Journal of Gay, Lesbian, and Bisexual Identity, 2*, 187-197.

41.   Brown, L. B., Sarosy, S. G., Cook, T. C., & Quarto, J. G. (1997). *Gay men and aging.* New York: Garland.

This book discusses findings on older gay men regarding their social life, relationships, sex life, and family life.

42.   Connolly, L. (1996). Long-term care and hospice: The special needs of older gay men and lesbians. *Journal of Gay & Lesbian Social Services, 5*(1), 77-91.

43.   Dorfman, R., Walters, K., Burke, P., Hardin, L., Karanik, T., Raphael, J., & Silverstein, E. (1995). Old, sad and alone: The myth of the aging homosexual. *Journal of Gerontological Social Work, 24*, 29-44.

This article reports findings from a survey of 108 older heterosexual, lesbian, and gay persons in urban California on depression, social support, and other variables.

44.   Grossman, A. H., D'Augelli, A. R., & Hershberger, S. L. (2000). Social support networks of lesbian, gay, and bisexual adults 60 years of age and older. *Journal of Gerontology, 55B*, 171-179.

45.   Herdt, G. H., Beeler, J., & Rawls, T. W. (1997). Life course diversity among older lesbians and gay men: A study in Chicago. *Journal of Gay, Lesbian, and Bisexual Identity, 2*, 231-246.

This article reports on a 10-month study of the lives and social and psychological needs of older lesbian and gay persons in Chicago.

46.   Jacobs, R. J., Rasmussen, L. A., & Hohman, M. M. (1999). The social support needs of older lesbians, gay men, and bisexuals. *Journal of Gay & Lesbian Social Services, 9*(1), 1-30.

47.   Kochman, A. (1997). Gay and lesbian elderly: Historical overview and implications for social work practice. *Journal of Gay & Lesbian Services, 6*(1), 1-10.

48.   Reid, J. D. (1995). Development in late life: Older lesbian and gay lives. In A. R. D'Augelli & C. J. Patterson (Eds.), *Lesbian, gay, and bisexual identities the over the lifespan: Psychological perspectives* (pp. 215-240). New York: Oxford University Press.

49.   Rosenfeld, D. (1999). Identity work among lesbian and gay elderly. *Journal of Aging Studies, 13*, 121-144

This article suggests that among gay and lesbian persons over age 65, there are unique subgroups with a variety of experiences because of ongoing social change and the importance of cohort effects on identity in this population.

50.   Shenk, D., & Fullmer, E. (1996). Significant relationships among older women: Cultural and personal constructions of lesbianism. *Journal of Women & Aging, 8*, 75-89.

51.   Wahler, J., & Gabbay, S. G. (1997). Gay male aging: A review of the literature. *Journal of Gay & Lesbian Social Services, 6*(3), 1-20.

52.   Whitford, G. S. (1997). Realities and hopes for older gay males. *Journal of Gay & Lesbian Social Services, 6*(1), 79-95.

IV. Selected Life Course Arenas

Coming Out—Identity Development

1. Barbone, S., & Rice, L. (1994). Coming out, being out, and acts of virtue. *Journal of Homosexuality, 27*(3/4), 91-110.

    This article examines three philosophical models for gay self-identity: utilitarianism, deontologism, and individualism.

2. Brown, L. S. (1995). Lesbian identities: Concepts and issues. In A. R. D'Augelli & C. J. Patterson (Eds.), *Lesbian, gay, and bisexual identities over the lifespan: Psychological perspectives* (pp. 3-23). New York: Oxford University Press.

3. Cass, V. C. (1996). Sexual orientation identity formation: A western phenomenon. In R. P. Cabaj & T. S. Stein (Eds.), *Textbook of homosexuality and mental health* (pp. 227-251). Washington, DC: American Psychiatric Press.

4. Chan, C. S. (1995). Issues of sexual identity in an ethnic minority: The case of Chinese American lesbians, gay men, and bisexual people. In A. R. D'Augelli & C. J. Patterson (Eds.), *Lesbian, gay, and bisexual identities over the lifespan* (pp. 87-101). New York: Oxford University Press.

5. Cohen, K. M., & Savin-Williams, R. C. (1996). Developmental perspectives on coming out to self and others. In R. C. Savin-Williams & K. M. Cohen (Eds.), *The lives of lesbians, gays, and bisexuals: Children to adults* (pp. 113-151). Fort Worth, TX: Harcourt Brace.

6. Courvant, D. (1999). Coming out disabled: A transsexual woman considers queer contributions to living with disability. *Journal of Gay, Lesbian, and Bisexual Identity, 4,* 97-105.

7. Cox, S., & Gallois, C. (1996). Gay and lesbian identity development: A social identity perspective. *Journal of Homosexuality, 30*(4), 1-30.

8. Cramer, E. P., & Gilson, S. F. (1999). Queers and crips: Parallel identity development processes for persons with nonvisible disabilities and lesbian, gay, and bisexual persons. *Journal of Gay, Lesbian, and Bisexual Identity, 4,* 23-37.

    This article critiques the limitations of identity development models for lgb persons and for persons with disabilities. Alternatively, it proposes an interactional identity development model.

9. Crisp, D., Priest, B., & Torgerson, A. (1998). African American gay men: Developmental issues, choices, and self-concept. *Family Therapy, 25,* 161-168.

10. D'Augelli, A. R. (1994). Identity development and sexual orientation: Toward a model of lesbian, gay, and bisexual development. In E. J. Trickett, R. J. Watts, & D. Birman (Eds.), *Human diversity: Prespectives on people in context* (pp. 312-333). San Francisco: Jossey-Bass.

    This chapter discusses how psychological views of identity reinforce heterosexist privilege.

11. Diamond, L. M. (1998). Development of sexual orientation among adolescent and young adult women. *Developmental Psychology, 34,* 1085-1095.

12. Dubé, E. M., & Savin-Williams, R. C. (1999). Sexual identity development among ethnic sexual-minority male youths. *Developmental Psychology, 35,* 1389-1398.

13. Eliason, M. J. (1996). Identity formation for lesbian, bisexual, and gay persons: Beyond a "minoritizing" view. *Journal of Homosexuality, 30*(3), 31-58.

    This article critiques existing concepts of identity and sexual identity, and it recommends a more comprehensive cyclical model of identity development that includes the variables of gender, race, and class.

14. Esterberg, K. G. (1997). *Lesbian and bisexual identities: Constructing communities, constructing selves.* Philadelphia: Temple University.

15. Fassinger, R. E., & Miller, B. A. (1996). Validation of an inclusive model of sexual minority identity formation on a sample of gay men. *Journal of Homosexuality, 32*(2), 53-78.

16. Fox, R. C. (1995). Bisexual identities. In A. R. D'Augelli & C. J. Patterson (Eds.), *Lesbian, gay, and bisexual identities over the lifespan: Psychological perspectives* (pp. 48-86). New York: Oxford University Press.

    This chapter examines the conception of bisexual identities according to a variety of theories, and reviews the research on bisexuality and bisexual identities. An important focus of this chapter is the multidimensionality of sexual orientation.

17. Gagné, P., Tewksbury, R., & McGaughey, D. (1997). Coming out and crossing over: Identity formation and proclamation in a transgender community. *Gender & Society, 11,* 478-508.

18. Golden, C. (1996). What's in a name? Sexual self-identification among women. In R. C. Savin-Williams & K. M. Cohen (Eds.), *The lives of lesbians, gays, and bisexuals: Children to adults* (pp. 229-249). Fort Worth, TX: Harcourt Brace.

    This chapter discusses the complications involved in adopting a lesbian identity.

19. Gonsiorek, J. C. (1995). Gay male identities: Concepts and issues. In A. R. D'Augelli & C. J. Patterson (Eds.), *Lesbians, gay, and bisexual identities over the life span* (pp. 24-47). New York: Oxford University Press.

20. Greene, B. (1998). Family, ethnic identity, and sexual orientation: African-American lesbians and gay men. In C. J. Patterson & A. R. D'Augelli (Eds.), *Lesbian, gay, and bisexual identities in families: Psychological perspectives* (pp. 40-52). New York: Oxford University Press.

21. Jackson, K., & Brown, L. B. (1996). Lesbians of African heritage: Coming out in the straight community. *Journal of Gay & Lesbian Social Services, 5*(4), 53-67.

22. Jensen, K. L. (1999). *Lesbian epiphanies: Women coming out in later life.* New York: Harrington Park Press.

23. Kessler, S. J., & McKenna, W. (2000). Gender construction in everyday life: Transsexualism. *Feminism & Psychology, 10*(1), 11-29.

24. Kitzinger, C., & Wilkinson, S. (1995). Transitions from heterosexuality to lesbianism: The discursive production of lesbian identities. *Developmental Psychology, 31*, 95-104.

This article examines women's accounts of their transition to a lesbian identity after previously identifying as heterosexual for a long time.

25. Levine, H. (1997). A further exploration of the lesbian identity developmental process and its measurement. *Journal of Homosexuality, 34*(2), 67-78.

26. Liu, P., & Chan, C. C. (1996). Lesbian, gay, and bisexual Asian Americans and their families. In J. Laird & R. J. Green (Eds.), *Lesbians and gays in couples and families: A handbook for therapists* (pp. 137-152). San Francisco: Jossey-Bass.

27. Manalansan, M. F. (1996). Double minorities: Latino, Black, and Asian men who have sex with men. In R. C. Savin-Williams & K. M. Cohen (Eds.), *The lives of lesbian, gay men, and bisexuals: Children to adults* (pp. 393-425). Fort Worth, TX: Harcourt Brace.

28. Marsiglia, F. F. (1998). Homosexuality and Latinos/as: Toward an integration of identities. *Journal of Gay & Lesbian Social Services, 8*(3), 113-125.

29. Martinez, D. G., & Sullivan, S. C. (1998). African American gay men and lesbians: Examining the complexity of gay identity development. *Journal of Human Behavior and the Social Environment, 1*, 243-264.

This article discusses identity development among African American gay and lesbian persons, and the multiple challenges they confront from African American communities and white gay and lesbian communities.

30. Meyer, S., & Schwitzer, A. M. (1999). Stages of identity development among college students with minority sexual orientation. *Journal of College Student Psychotherapy, 13*, 41-64.

31. Morris, J. F. (1997). Lesbian coming out as a multidimensional process. *Journal of Homosexuality, 33*(2), 1-22.

32. Parks, C. (1999). Lesbian identity development: An examination of differences across generations. *American Journal of Orthopsychiatry, 69*, 347-361.

33. Rodriguez, R. A. (1996). Clinical issues in identity development in gay Latino men. In C. J. Alexander (Ed.), *Gay and lesbian mental health: A source book for practitioners* (pp. 127-157). New York: Harrington Park Press.

34. Rust, P. C. (1996). Finding a sexual identity and community: Therapeutic implications and cultural assumptions in scientific models of coming out. In E. D. Rothblum & L. A. Bond (Eds.), *Preventing heterosexism and homophobia* (pp. 87-123). Thousand Oaks, CA: Sage Publications.

This chapter discusses linear models of coming out and their advantages and limitations in use with clients.

35. Stokes, J. P., Damon, W., & McKirnan, D. J. (1997). Predictors of movement toward homosexuality: A longitudinal study of bisexual men. *The Journal of Sex Research, 34*, 304-312.

36. Walters, K. L. (1997). Urban lesbian and gay American Indian identity: Implications for mental health service delivery. *Journal of Gay & Lesbian Social Services, 6*(2), 43-65.

37. Weinberg, M. S., Williams, C. J., & Pryor, D. W. (1998). Becoming and being "bisexual." In E. J. Haeberle & R. Gindorf (Eds.), *Bisexualities: The ideology and practice of sexual contact with both men and women* (pp. 169-181). New York: Continuum.

Coming Out—Disclosure

38. Badgett, M. V. (1996). Employment and sexual orientation: Disclosure and discrimination in the workplace. *Journal of Gay & Lesbian Social Services, 4*(4), 29-52.

39. Beeler, J., & DiProva, V. (1999). Family adjustment following disclosure of homosexuality by a member: Themes discerned in narrative accounts. *Journal of Marital and Family Therapy, 25*, 443-459.

    This article addresses how families respond to disclosure of a gay or lesbian family member over time and how they integrate this family member and his or her relationships into the family.

40. Ben-Ari, A. (1995). The discovery that an offspring is gay: Parents', gay men's, and lesbians' perspectives. *Journal of Homosexuality, 30*(1), 89-112.

41. Bliss, G. K., & Harris, M. B. (1998). Experiences of gay and lesbian teachers and parents with coming out in a school setting. *Journal of Gay & Lesbian Social Services, 8*(2), 13-28.

42. Boon, S. D., & Miller, R. J. (1999). Exploring the links between interpersonal trust and the reasons underlying gay and bisexual males' disclosure of their sexual orientation to their mothers. *Journal of Homosexuality, 37*(3), 45-68.

43. Bragg, K. (1997). Being a gay or lesbian professional in a psychiatric hospital for adolescents. *Journal of Gay & Lesbian Social Services, 6*(4), 25-38.

    This article examines the style and degree of disclosure to staff, clients, and family by several staff persons at one inpatient setting.

44. D'Augelli, A. R., Hershberger, S. L., & Pilkington, N. W. (1998). Lesbian, gay, and bisexual youth and their families: Disclosure of sexual orientation and its consequences. *American Journal of Orthopsychiatry, 68*, 361-371.

45. Driscoll, J. M., Kelley, F. A., & Fassinger, R. E. (1996). Lesbian identity and disclosure in the workplace: Relation to occupational stress and satisfaction. *Journal of Vocational Behavior, 48*, 229-242.

46. Ellis, A. L., & Riggle, E. D. (1995). The relation of job satisfaction and degree of openness about one's sexual orientation for lesbians and gay men. *Journal of Homosexuality, 30*(2), 75-85.

47. Fish, R. C. (1997). Coming out issues of gay and lesbian mental health professionals in voluntary and involuntary settings. *Journal of Gay & Lesbian Social Services, 6*(4), 11-24.

48. Fullmer, E. M., Shenk, D., & Eastland, L. J. (1999). Negating identity: A feminist analysis of the social invisibility of older lesbians, *Journal of Women & Aging, 11*, 131-148.

49. Holtzen, D. W., Kenny, M. E., & Mahalik, J. R. (1995). Contributions of parental attachment to gay or lesbian disclosure to parents and dysfunctional cognitive processes. *Journal of Counseling Psychology, 42,* 350-355.

50. Hunt, S., & Main, T. L. (1997). Sexual orientation confusion among spouses of transvestites and transsexuals following disclosure of spouse's gender dysphoria. *Journal of Psychology and Human Sexuality, 9*(2), 39-52.

51. Jones, B. E., & Hill, M. J. (1996). African American lesbians, gay men, and bisexuals. In R. P. Cabaj & T. S. Stein (Eds.), *Textbook of homosexuality and mental health* (pp. 549-561). Washington, DC: American Psychiatric Press.

     This chapter discusses obstacles that exist in African American and gay and lesbian communities for identity development and disclosure by African American glb persons.

52. Jordan, K. M., & Deluty, R. H. (1998). Coming out for lesbian women: Its relation to anxiety, positive affectivity, self-esteem, and social support. *Journal of Homosexuality, 35*(2), 41-63.

     This article reports on a study of the association between lesbians' disclosure of their sexual orientation and psychological adjustment.

53. Lynch, J. M., & Murray, K. (2000). For the love of the children: The coming out process for lesbian and gay parents and stepparents. *Journal of Homosexuality, 39*(1), 1-24.

54. Martinson, J. C., Fisher, D. G., & DeLapp, T. D. (1996). Client disclosure of lesbianism: A challenge for health care providers. *Journal of Gay & Lesbian Social Services, 4*(3), 81-94.

     This article reports on a large survey of lesbians that focused on differences among the characteristics and health care experiences of those who disclosed to a health care provider and those who did not do so.

55. Mays, V. M., Chaters, L. M., Cochran, S. D., & Mackness, J. (1998). African American families in diversity: Gay men and lesbians as participants in family networks. *Journal of Comparative Family Studies, 29,* 73-87.

     This article discusses disclosure decisions and issues for African American gay and lesbian persons concerning members of their family of origin and extended family members, as well as the reactions they receive from family members.

56. Merighi, J. R., & Grimes, M. D. (2000). Coming out to families in a multicultural context. *Families in Society, 81,* 32-41.

57. Miller, R. J., & Boon, S. D. (2000). Trust and disclosure of sexual orientation in gay males' mother-son relationships. *Journal of Homosexuality, 38*(3), 41-63.

58. Oswald, R. F. (2000). Family and friendship relationships after young women come out as bisexual or lesbian. *Journal of Homosexuality, 38*(3), 65-83.

59. Radonsky, V. E., & Borders, L. D. (1995). Factors influencing lesbians' direct disclosure of their sexual orientation. *Journal of Gay & Lesbian Psychotherapy, 2*(3), 17-37.

60. Savin-Williams, R. C. (1998). The disclosure to families of same-sex attractions by lesbian, gay, and bisexual youths. *Journal of Research on Adolescence, 8,* 49-68.

61. Savin-Williams, R. C. (1998). Lesbian, gay, and bisexual youths' relationships with their parents. In C. J. Patterson & A. R. D'Augelli (Eds.), *Lesbian, gay, and bisexual identities in families: Psychological perspectives* (pp. 75-98). New York: Oxford University Press.

This chapter examines the significance of parents to glb youths, whether these youths make disclosures to parents, reasons why they should not do so, and associations between disclosures to parents and youths' psychological health.

62. Savin-Williams, R. C., & Dubé, E. M. (1998). Parental reactions to their child's disclosure of a gay/lesbian identity. *Family Relations, 47,* 7-13.

63. Scott, R. R., & Ortiz, E. T. (1996). Marriage and coming out: Four patterns in homosexual males. *Journal of Gay & Lesbian Social Services, 4*(3), 67-79.

64. Tiemann, K. A., Kennedy, S. A., & Haga, M. P. (1998). Rural lesbians' strategies for coming out to health care professionals. In C. M. Ponticelli (Ed.), *Gateways to improving lesbian health and health care: Opening doors* (pp. 61-75.). New York: Harrington Park Press.

65. Waldner, L. K., & Magruder, B. (1999). Coming out to parents: Perceptions of family relations, perceived resources, and identity expression as predictors of identity disclosure for gay and lesbian adolescents. *Journal of Homosexuality, 37*(2), 83-100.

66. Waldo, C. R. (1998). Out on campus: Sexual orientation and academic climate in a university context. *American Journal of Community Psychology, 26,* 745-774.

67. Waldo, C. R., & Kemp, J. L. (1997). Should I come out to my students? An empirical investigation. *Journal of Homosexuality, 34*(2), 79-94.

68. Williamson, D. S. (1998). Disclosure is a family event. *Family Relations, 47,* 23-25.

Friendships

69. Diamond, L. M. (2000). Passionate friendships among adolescent sexual-minority women. *Journal of Research on Adolescence, 10,* 191-209.

This article reports findings on close adolescent friendships among 80 lesbian, bisexual, and unlabeled women, ages 18-25.

70. Nardi, P. M. (1999). *Gay men's friendships: Invincible communities.* Chicago: University of Chicago Press.

71. Nardi, P. M., & Sherrod, D. (1994). Friendship in the lives of gay men and lesbians. *Journal of Social and Personal Relationships, 11,* 185-199.

72. Weinstock, J. S., & Rothblum, E. D. (1996). *Lesbian friendships: For ourselves and each other.* New York: New York University.

Couples

73.   Alexander, C. J. (1997). Factors contributing to the termination of long-term gay male relationships. *Journal of Gay and Lesbian Social Services, 7*(1), 1-12.

74.   Baccman, C., Folkesson, P., & Norlander, T. (1999). Expectations of romantic relationships: A comparison between homosexual and heterosexual men with regard to Baxter's criteria. *Social Behavior and Personality, 27*, 363-374.

75.   Bailey, J. M., Kim, P. Y., Hills, A., & Linsenmeier, J. A. (1997). Butch, femme, or straight-acting? Partner preferences of gay men and lesbians. *Journal of Personality and Social Psychology, 73*, 960-973.

76.   Bryant, S., & Demian (1994). Relationship characteristics of American gay and lesbian couples: Findings from a national survey. *Journal of Gay & Lesbian Social Services, 1*(2), 101-117.

      This article reports on a survey of 1,749 self-selected gay and lesbian persons representing 560 gay couples and 706 lesbian couples.

77.   Cabaj, R., & Purcell, D. W. (Eds.). (1997). *On the road to the same-sex marriage: A supportive guide to psychological, political, and legal issues.* San Francisco: Jossey-Bass.

78.   Card, C. (1997). Against marriage. In J. Corvino (Ed.), *Same sex: The ethics, science and culture of homosexuality* (pp. 317-382). Lanham, MD: Rowman & Littlefield.

      This chapter discusses gay and lesbian marriage from a lesbian-feminist perspective. The author opposes both gay and lesbian and heterosexual marriage because of the moral cost of involvement of the state.

79.   Caron, S. L., & Ulin, M. (1997). Closeting and the quality of lesbian relationships. *Families in Society, 78*, 413-419.

80.   Carrington, D. (1999). *Home: Relationships and family life among lesbians and gay men.* Chicago: University of Chicago Press.

81.   Carroll, L., Hoenigmann-Stovall, N., Turner, J. A., & Gilroy, P. (1999). A comparative study of relational interconnectedness, merger, and ego development in lesbian, gay male, and heterosexual couples. *Journal of Gay & Lesbian Social Services, 9*(1), 51-67.

82.   Causby, V., Lockhart, L., White, B., & Greene, K. (1995). Fusion and conflict resolution in lesbian relationships. *Journal of Gay & Lesbian Social Services, 3*(1), 67-83.

83.   Esterberg, K. G. (1994). Being a lesbian and being in love: Constructing identity through relationships. *Journal of Gay & Lesbian Social Services, 1*(2), 57-82.

      This article reports on a study on 94 lesbian and bisexual women concerning the ways in which they construct their identity, and the role of relationships in their identity construction.

84.   Greene, K., Causby, V., & Miller, D. H. (1999). The nature and function of fusion in the dynamics of lesbian relationships. *Affilia, 14*, 78-97.

85.   Hill, C. A. (1999). Fusion and conflict in lesbian relationships? *Feminism & Psychology, 9*, 179-185.

86. James, S. E., & Murphy, B. C. (1998). Gay and lesbian relationships in a changing social context. In C. J. Patterson & A. R. D'Augelli (Eds.), *Lesbian, gay, and bisexual identities in families: Psychological perspectives* (pp. 99-121). New York: Oxford University Press.

This chapter examines the psychological, social, and political contexts that affect gay and lesbian couples.

87. Julien, D., Arellano, C., & Turgeon, L. (1997). Gender issues in heterosexual, gay and lesbian couples. In W. K. Halford & H. J. Markman (Eds.), *Clinical handbook of marriage and couples intervention* (pp. 107-127). New York: Wiley.

88. Julien, D., Chartrand, E., & Began, J. (1999). Social networks, structural interdependence, and conjugal adjustment in heterosexual, gay, and lesbian couples. *Journal of Marriage and the Family, 61*, 516-530.

89. Keeler, W. A. (1999). Growth inducing conflict resolution strategies as a means of reducing the effect of discordant outness on relationship satisfaction. *Journal of Gay & Lesbian Social Services, 10*(2), 1-31.

90. Kitzinger, C., & Coyle, A. (1995). Lesbian and gay couples: Speaking of difference. *The Psychologist, 8*, 64-69.

91. Klinger, R. L. (1996). Lesbian couples. In R. P. Cabaj & T. S. Stein (Eds.), *Textbook of homosexuality and mental health* (pp. 339-352). Washington, DC: American Psychiatric Press.

92. Klinkenberg, D., & Rose, S. (1994). Dating scripts of gay men and lesbians. *Journal of Homosexuality, 26*(4), 23-35.

93. Kurdek, L. A. (1994). Areas of conflict for gay, lesbian, and heterosexual cohabiting couples: What couples argue about influences relationship satisfaction. *Journal of Marriage and the Family, 56*, 923-934.

94. Kurdek, L. A. (1995). Developing changes in relationship quality in gay and lesbian cohabiting couples. *Developmental Psychology, 31*, 86-94.

95. Kurdek, L. A. (1995). Lesbian and gay couples. In A. R. D'Augelli & C. J. Patterson (Eds.), *Lesbian, gay, and bisexual identities over the lifespan: Psychological perspectives* (pp. 243-251). New York: Oxford University Press.

This chapter summarizes descriptions of lesbian and gay couples and theory-based findings on relationship satisfaction and stability among them.

96. Kurdek, L. A. (1996). The deterioration of relationship quality for gay and lesbian cohabitating couples: A five-year prospective longitudinal study. *Personal Relationships, 3*, 417-442.

97. Kurdek, L. A. (1997). Adjustment to relationship dissolution in gay, lesbian, and heterosexual partners. *Personal Relationships, 4*, 145-161.

98. Kurdek, L. A. (1997). Relation between neuroticism and dimensions of relationship commitment: Evidence from gay, lesbian, and heterosexual couples. *Journal of Family Psychology, 11*, 109-124.

99. Kurdek, L. A. (1998). Relationship outcomes and their predictors: Longitudinal evidence from heterosexual married, gay cohabiting, and lesbian cohabiting couples. *Journal of Marriage and the Family, 60*, 553-568.

100. LaSala, M. C. (2000). Gay male couples: The importance of coming out and being out to parents. *Journal of Homosexuality, 39*(2), 47-71.

101. Matteson, D. R. (1999). Intimate bisexual couples. In J. Carlson & L. Sperry (Eds.), *The intimate couple* (pp. 439-459). Philadelphia: Taylor & Francis.

102. Metz, M. E., Simon Rosser, B. R., & Strapko, N. (1994). Differences in conflict-resolution styles among heterosexual, gay, and lesbian couples. *Journal of Sex Research, 31,* 298-308.

103. Mohr, J. J. (1999). Same-sex romantic attachment. In J. Cassidy & P. R. Phillips (Eds.), *Handbook of attachment: Theory, research, and clinical applications* (pp. 378-394). New York: Guilford.

104. Oberton, S. (1998). Reclaiming the "housewife": Lesbians and household work. *Journal of Lesbian Studies, 2,* 69-83.

105. Ortiz, E., & Scott, P. (1994). Gay husbands and fathers: Reasons for marriage among homosexual men. *Journal of Gay & Lesbian Social Services, 1*(1), 59-71.

   This paper explores the motivations for marriage among 15 gay men who were currently or formerly married to women.

106. Patterson, D. G., & Schwartz, P. (1994). The social construction of conflict in intimate same-sex couples. In D. D. Cahn (Ed.), *Conflict in personal relationships* (pp. 3-26). Hillsdale, NJ: Laurence Erlbaum.

107. Robinson, C. H. (1997). Everyday [hetero]sexism: Strategies of resistance and lesbian couples. In C. R. Ronai, B. A. Zsembik, & J. R. Feagan (Eds.), *Everyday sexism in the third millennium* (pp. 33-50). New York: Routledge.

   This article discusses how African American and interracial lesbian couples resist heterosexism in everyday life.

108. Rosenbluth, S. C., & Steil, J. M. (1995). Predictors of intimacy for women in heterosexual and homosexual couples. *Journal of Social and Personal Relationships, 12,* 163-175.

109. Savin-Williams, R. C. (1996). Dating and romantic relationships among gay, lesbian, and bisexual youth. In R. C. Savin-Williams & K. M. Cohen (Eds.), *The lives of lesbian, gay men, and bisexuals: Children to adults* (pp. 166-180). Fort Worth, TX: Harcourt Brace.

110. Slater, S. (1994). Approaching and avoiding the work of the middle years: Affairs in committed lesbian relationships. *Women & Therapy, 15,* 19-34.

   This article discusses the experience of lesbian couples when one of the partners develops a serious outside attraction while the couple is deliberating a permanent relational commitment.

111. Smith, R. G., & Brown, R. A. (1998). The impact of social support on gay male couples. *Journal of Homosexuality, 33,* 39-61.

112. Stearns, D. C., & Sabini, J. (1997). Dyadic adjustment and community involvement in same-sex couples. *Journal of Gay, Lesbian, and Bisexual Identity, 2,* 265-283.

113. Tully, C. T. (1994). To boldly go where no one has gone before: The legalization of lesbian and gay marriages. *Journal of Gay & Lesbian Social Services, 1*(1), 73-87.

This article provides an historical account of the concepts of marriage and family, current definitions, legislative and judicial responses to lesbian and gay marriage, and a case for these marriages.

114. Williams, W. L. (1998). Social acceptance of same-sex relationships in families: Models from other cultures. In C. J. Patterson & A. R. D'Augelli (Eds.), *Lesbian, gay, and bisexual identities in families: Psychological perspectives* (pp. 53-71). New York: Oxford University Press.

115. Zak, A., & McDonald, C. (1997). Satisfaction and trust in intimate relationships: Do lesbians and heterosexual women differ? *Psychological Reports, 80,* 904-906.

Families

116. Allen, K. R., & Demo, D. H. (1995). The families of lesbians and gay men: A new frontier in family research. *Journal of Marriage and the Family, 57,* 111-127.

117. Allen, M., & Burrell, N. (1996). Comparing the impact of homosexual and heterosexual parents on children: Meta-analysis of existing research. *Journal of Homosexuality, 32*(2), 19-35.

118. Arnup, K. (1999). Out in this world: The social and legal context of gay and lesbian families. *Journal of Gay & Lesbian Social Services, 10*(1), 1-25.

119. Bailey, J. M., Bobrow, D., Wolfe, M., & Mikach, S. (1995). Sexual orientation of adult sons of gay fathers. *Developmental Psychology, 31,* 124-129.

120. Bigner, J. J. (1999). Raising our sons: Gay men as fathers. *Journal of Gay & Lesbian Social Services, 10*(1), 61-77.

This article compares parenting abilities and styles of gay and non-gay fathers, especially those raising sons.

121. Bigner, J. J. (2000). Gay and lesbian families. In W. C. Nichols (Ed.), *Handbook of family development and intervention* (pp. 279-298). New York: Wiley.

122. Chambers, D. L., & Polikoff, N. D. (1999). Family law and gay and lesbian family issues in the twentieth century. *Family Law Quarterly, 33,* 523-542.

123. Chan, R. W., Raboy, B., & Patterson, C. J. (1998). The psychosocial adjustment among children conceived via donor insemination by lesbian and heterosexual mothers. *Child Development, 69,* 443-457.

This article reports on associations among family structure, family processes, and the psychological adjustment of children conceived through donor insemination.

124. Demo, D. H., & Allen, K. R. (1996). Diversity within lesbian and gay families: Challenges and implications for family theory and research. *Journal of Social and Personal Relationships, 13,* 415-434.

125. Falk, P. J. (1997). Lesbian mothers: Psychosocial assumptions in family law. *Journal of Lesbian Studies, 1,* 37-54.

126. Fitzgerald, B. (1999). Children of lesbian and gay parents: A review of the literature. *Marriage and Family Review, 29,* 57-75.

This article reviews the research literature on children of both divorced gay and lesbian parents and planned gay and lesbian families.

127. Flaks, D. K., Fisher, I., Masterpasqua, F., & Joseph, G. (1995). Lesbians choosing motherhood: A comparative study of lesbian and heterosexual parents and their children. *Developmental Psychology, 31,* 105-114.

128. Fredriksen, K. I. (1999). Family caregiving responsibilities among lesbians and gay men. *Social Work, 44,* 142-155.

129. Hare, J. (1994). Concerns and issues faced by families headed by a lesbian couple. *Families in Society, 75,* 27-35

130. Johnson, T. W., & Keren, M. S. (1998). The families of lesbian women and gay men. In M. McGoldrick (Ed.), *Re-visioning family therapy: Race, culture, and gender in clinical practice* (pp. 320-329). New York: Guilford.

131. Laird, J. (Ed.). (1999). *Lesbians and lesbian families: Reflections on theory and practice.* New York: Columbia University Press.

132. McNeill, K. L., Rienzi, B. M., & Kposowa, A. (1998). Families and parenting: A comparison of lesbian and heterosexual mothers. *Psychological Reports, 82,* 59-62.

133. Nations, L. (1997). Lesbian mothers: A descriptive study of a distinctive family structure. *Journal of Gay & Lesbian Social Services, 7*(1), 23-47.

134. Nelson, F. (1999). Achieving motherhood. *Journal of Gay & Lesbian Social Services, 10*(1), 27-46.

This article focuses on the unique experiences of motherhood for lesbians, different types of lesbian families, and needs for social and community services among lesbian mothers.

135. Parks, C. A. (1998). Lesbian parenthood: A review of the literature. *American Journal of Orthopsychiatry, 68,* 376-389.

This article reviews findings from studies of lesbian families with children from 1980 to 1996.

136. Patterson, C. J. (1994). Children of the lesbian baby boom: Behavioral adjustment, self-concept, and sex role identity. In B. Greene & G. M. Herek (Eds.), *Lesbian and gay psychology: Theory, research, and clinical applications* (pp. 156-175). Thousand Oaks, CA: Sage Publications.

137. Patterson, C. J. (1995). Families of the lesbian baby boom: Parents' division of labor and children's adjustment. *Developmental Psychology, 31,* 115-123.

This article reports a study on 26 families headed by lesbian couples, focusing on their division of labor and satisfaction with their relationships, and their children's psychosocial adjustment.

138. Patterson, C. J. (1997). Children of lesbian and gay parents. *Advances in Clinical Child Psychology, 19,* 235-281.

This chapter reviews research on the personal and social development of children of lesbian and gay parents.

139. Patterson, C. J. (1998). The family lives of children born to lesbian mothers. In C. J. Patterson & A. R. D'Augelli (Eds.), *Lesbian, gay, and bisexual identities in families: Psychological perspectives* (pp. 154-176). New York: Oxford University Press.

140. Patterson, C. J., & Chan, R. W. (1996). Gay fathers and their children. In R. P. Cabaj & T. S. Stein (Eds.), *Textbook of homosexuality and mental health* (pp. 371-393). Washington, DC: American Psychiatric Press.

141. Patterson, C. J., Hurt, S., & Mason, C. D. (1998). Families of the lesbian baby boom: Children's contact with grandparents and other adults. *American Journal of Orthopsychiatry, 68*, 390-399.

142. Shernoff, M. (1996). Gay men choosing to be fathers. *Journal of Gay & Lesbian Social Services, 4*(2), 41-54.

143. Sullivan, M. (1996). Rozzie and Harriet? Gender and family patterns of lesbian co-parents. *Gender & Society, 10*, 747-767.

144. Tasker, F. (1999). Children in lesbian-led families: A review. *Clinical Child Psychology and Psychiatry, 4*, 153-166.

145. Tasker, F., & Golombok, S. (1995). Adults raised as children in lesbian families. *American Journal of Orthopsychiatry, 65*, 203-215.

This article reports results of a longitudinal study of 25 young adults raised in lesbian families and 21 others raised by heterosexual single mothers.

146. Van Voorhis, R., & McClain, L. (1997). Accepting a lesbian mother. *Families in Society, 79*, 642-650.

Work

147. Anastas, J. W. (1998). Working against discrimination: Gay, lesbian and bisexual people on the job. *Journal of Gay & Lesbian Social Services, 8*(3), 83-89.

148. Boatwright, K. J., Gilbert, M. S., Forrest, L., & Ketzenberger, K. (1996). Impact of identity development upon career trajectory: Listening to the voices of lesbian women. *Journal of Vocational Behavior, 48*, 210-228.

149. Chung, Y. B. & Harmon, L. W. (1994). The career interests and aspirations of gay men: How sex-role orientation is related. *Journal of Vocational Behavior, 45*, 223-239.

150. Croteau, J. M. (1996). Research on the work experiences of lesbian, gay, and bisexual people: An integrative review of methodology and findings. *Journal of Vocational Behavior, 48*, 195-209.

This article reviews the methodology and content of nine studies on the workplace experiences of glb persons.

151. Ellis, A. L. (1996). Sexual identity issues in the workplace: Past and present. *Journal of Gay & Lesbian Social Services, 4*(4), 1-15.

152. Fassinger, R. E. (1995). From invisibility to integration: Lesbian identity in the workplace. *Career Development Quarterly, 44*, 148-166.

153. Lonborg, S. D., & Phillips, J. M. (1996). Investigating the career development of gay, lesbian, and bisexual people: Methodological considerations and recommendations. *Journal of Vocational Behavior, 48*, 176-194.

This article focuses on understanding career development of glb persons using both qualitative and quantitative methods. It examines within-group and between-group differences in career-related cognitions and experiences.

154. Myrick, R., & Brown, M. H. (1998). Out of the closet and into the classroom: A survey of lesbian, gay, and bisexual educators' classroom strategies and experiences in colleges and universities. *Journal of Gay, Lesbian, and Bisexual Identity, 3,* 295-317.

155. Pope, M. (1996). Gay and lesbian career counseling: Special career counseling issues. *Journal of Gay & Lesbian Social Services, 4*(4), 91-105.

156. Shallenberger, D. (1994). Professional and openly gay: A narrative study of the experience. *Journal of Management Inquiry, 3,* 119-142.

157. Sussman, T. (1996). Gay men in the workplace: Issues for mental health counselors. *Journal of Gay, Lesbian, and Bisexual Identity, 1,* 193-211.

Spirituality

158. Baez, E. J. (1996). Spirituality and the gay Latino client. *Journal of Gay & Lesbian Social Services, 4*(2), 69-81.

    This article discusses the importance of understanding and acknowledging the role of spiritual beliefs and practices when working with gay Latinos.

159. Barret, R., & Barzan, R. (1996). Spiritual experiences of gay men and lesbians. *Counseling and Values, 41,* 4-15.

160. Booth, L. (1995). Spirituality and the gay community. *Journal of Gay & Lesbian Social Services, 2*(1), 57-65.

161. Haldeman, D. C. (1996). Spirituality and religion in the lives of lesbians and gay men. In R. P. Cabaj & T. S. Stein (Eds.), *Textbook of homosexuality and mental health* (pp. 881-896). Washington, DC: American Psychiatric Press.

162. Helmniak, D. A. (1997). The Bible on homosexuality: Ethically neutral. In J. Corvino (Ed.), *Same sex: The ethics, science and culture of homosexuality* (pp. 81-104). Lanham, MD: Rowman & Littlefield.

163. Shallenberger, D. (1998). *Reclaiming the spirit: Gay men and lesbians come to terms with religion.* New Brunswick, NJ: Rutgers University Press.

164. Wagner, G., Serafini, J., Rabkin, J., Remien, R., & Willians, J. (1994). Integration of one's religion and homosexuality: A weapon against internalized homophobia. *Journal of Homosexuality, 26*(4), 91-110.

    This article reports on a study of the association between internalized homophobia and integration of one's religious faith with one's sexual orientation.

165. Yip, A. K. (1999). The politics of counter-rejection: Gay Christians and the church. *Journal of Homosexuality, 37*(2), 47-63.

    This article discusses the accounts of 60 gay men in managing the stigma they experience in Christian churches.

V. Health

General Health Issues

1. Ettelbrick, P. L. (1996). Legal issues in health care for lesbians and gay men. *Journal of Gay & Lesbian Social Services, 5*(1), 93-109.

2. Faria, G. (1997). The challenge of health care social work with gay men and lesbians. *Social Work in Health Care, 25(1-2),* 65-72.

    This article discusses how heterosexism in health care delivery systems may affect lesbian and gay clients, and describes how social workers in health care settings can intervene in unbiased ways on their behalf.

3. Kauth, M. R., Hartwig, M. J., & Kalichman, S. C. (2000). Health behavior relevant to psychotherapy with lesbian, gay, and bisexual clients. In R. M. Perez & K. A. DeBord (Eds.), *Handbook of counseling and psychotherapy with lesbian, gay, and bisexual clients* (pp. 435-456). Washington, DC: American Psychological Association.

    This chapter summarizes the literature on access to health care, utilization of health care services, health risk behaviors, and wellness and health-promoting efforts among lesbian, gay, and bisexual adults.

4. National Lesbian and Gay Health Association. (1997). Removing barriers to healthcare for lesbian, gay, bisexual, and transgender clients: A model provider education program and participant resource guide. Washington, DC: Author.

5. Schwartz, M. (1996). Gay men and the health care system. *Journal of Gay & Lesbian Social Services, 5*(1), 19-32.

GLBT Youth Health Issues

6. Allen, L. B., Glicken, A. D., Beach, R. K., & Naylor, K. E. (1998). Adolescent health care experience of gay, lesbian, and bisexual young adults. *Journal of Adolescent Health, 23,* 212-220.

    This article reports on a survey of lesbian, gay, and bisexual youth regarding their experience with health care providers, especially focusing on the issue of medical confidentiality. It reports on participants' suggestions for improving care.

7. Dempsey, C. (1994). Health and social issues of gay, lesbian, and bisexual adolescents. *Families in Society, 75,* 160-167.

8. Garofalo, R., Wolf, R. C., Kessel, S., Palfrey, S. J., & DuRant, R. H. (1998). The association between health risk behaviors and sexual orientation among a school-based sample of adolescents. *Pediatrics, 101,* 895-902.

9. Hunter, J., & Schaecher, R. (1994). AIDS prevention for lesbian, gay, and bisexual adolescents. *Families in Society, 75,* 346-354.

10. Rotheram-Borus, M. J., Reid, H., Rosario, M., & Kasen, S. (1995). Determinants of safer sex patterns among gay/bisexual male adolescents. *Journal of Adolescence, 18,* 3-15.

11. Ryan, C., & Futterman, D. (1998). *Lesbian and gay youth: Care and counseling.* New York: Columbia University Press.

   This book is a comprehensive reference manual on the physical and mental health needs of youth who are lesbian, gay, or questioning their sexual orientation. It includes guidelines for assessment and intervention for a wide variety of health-related conditions.

12. Saewyc, E. M., Bearinger, L. H., Heinz, P. A., Blum, R. W., & Resnick, M. D. (1998). Gender differences in health and risk behaviors among bisexual and homosexual adolescents. *Journal of Adolescent Health, 23,* 181-188.

13. Wright, E. R., Gonzalez, C., Werner, J. N., Laughner, S. T., & Wallace, M. (1998). Indiana Youth Access Project: A model for responding to the HIV risk behaviors of gay, lesbian, and bisexual youth in the heartland. *Journal of Adolescent Health, 23*(2 supplement), 83-95.

Transgender Health Issues

14. Bockting, W. O., Robinson, B. E., & Rosser, B. R. (1999). Transgender HIV prevention: A qualitative needs assessment. *AIDS Care, 10,* 505-526.

   This article reports on focus groups of transgender individuals regarding their HIV-related risks and prevention needs. It also reviews literature on HIV/AIDS prevalence, risk behaviors, prevention knowledge and attitudes, and prevention strategies used among transgender populations.

15. Bockting, W. O., Rosser, B. R., & Scheltema, K. (1999). Transgender HIV prevention: Implementation and evaluation of a workshop. *Health Education Research, 14,* 177-183.

16. Grimaldi, J. (2000). HIV care for male-to-female pre-operative transsexuals. In M. Shernoff (Ed.), *AIDS and mental health practice: Clinical and policy issues* (pp. 159-186). New York: Haworth Press.

Lesbian & Bisexual Women's Health Issues

17. Axtell, S. (1999). Disability and chronic illness identity: Interviews with lesbians and bisexual women and their partners. *Journal of Gay, Lesbian, and Bisexual Identity, 4,* 53-72.

   This article discusses results from interviews with lesbian and bisexual women with disabilities or chronic illnesses, focusing on challenges to identity, relationships, and community building.

18. Butler, S. S., & Hope, B. (1999). Health and well-being for late middle-aged and old lesbians in a rural area. *Journal of Gay & Lesbian Social Services, 9*(4), 27-46.

   This article reports on a study that used naturalistic interviews to examine the health care experiences of older lesbians living in a rural area of the U.S. It discusses the policy and practice implications of the findings.

19. Einhorn, L., & Polgar, M. (1994). HIV-risk behavior among lesbians and bisexual women. *AIDS Education and Prevention, 6(6),* 514-523.

20. Gomez, C. A. (1995). Lesbians at risk for HIV: The unresolved debate. In G. M. Herek & B. Greene (Eds.), *AIDS, identity, and community: The HIV epidemic and lesbians and gay men* (pp. 19-31). Thousand Oaks, CA: Sage Publications.

21. Kunkel, L. E., & Skokan, L. A. (1998). Factors which influence cervical cancer screening among lesbians. *Journal of the Gay and Lesbian Medical Association, 2,* 7-15.

    This article reports on a survey of the Health Belief Model and its association with cervical screening guideline compliance among lesbians. It focuses on the importance of self-efficacy and availability of information as predictors of compliance.

22. Levy, E. (1996). Reproductive issues for lesbians. *Journal of Gay & Lesbian Social Services, 5*(1), 49-58.

23. Norman, A. D., Perry, M. J., Stevenson, L. Y., Kelly, J. A., & Roffman, R. A. (1996). Lesbian and bisexual women in small cities—At risk for HIV? *Public Health Reports, 111,* 347-351.

24. Peterson, K. J., & Bricker-Jenkins, M. (1996). Lesbians and the health care system. *Journal of Gay & Lesbian Social Services, 5*(1), 33-47.

    This article reviews the literature on the attitudes of health care providers toward lesbian recipients, health care seeking behaviors of lesbians, the barriers they encounter, and their preferences for providers. It makes recommendations for social workers in health care.

25. Rankow, E. J. (1997). Lesbian health issues and cultural sensitivity training for providers in the primary care setting: Results of a pilot intervention. *Journal of the Gay and Lesbian Medical Association, 1,* 227-234.

26. Rankow, E. J., & Tessaro, I. (1998). Mammography and risk factors for breast cancer in lesbian and bisexual women. *American Journal of Health Behavior, 22,* 403-410.

    This article reports on a survey of risk factors and screening adherence in a sample of lesbian and bisexual women. It discusses the role of economic barriers to screening behaviors, and compares rates of nulliparity and alcohol use to other samples of women.

27. Roberts, S. J., & Sorenson, L. (1999). Health related behaviors and cancer screening of lesbians: Results from the Boston Lesbian Health Project. *Women and Health, 28*(4), 1-12.

28. Saulnier, C. F. (1999). Choosing a health care provider: A community survey of what is important to lesbians. *Families in Society, 80,* 254-262.

    This article reports on a large survey of lesbians and bisexual women that focused on the qualities of physical and mental health care providers that were important to them. It includes some specific recommendations for practitioners based on the findings.

29. Shotsky, W. J. (1996). Women who have sex with other women: HIV seroprevalence in New York State counseling and testing programs. *Women and Health, 24*(2), 1-15.

30. Stevens, P. E. (1993). Lesbians and HIV: Clinical, research, and policy issues. *American Journal of Orthopsychiatry, 63,* 289-294.

31. Stevens, P. E. (1996). Lesbians and doctors: Experiences of solidarity and domination in health care settings. *Gender and Society, 10*(1), 24-41.

32. Stevens, P. E., & Hall, J. M. (1990). Abusive health care interactions experienced by lesbians: A case of institutional violence in the treatment of women. *Response, 13*(3), 23-27.

33. Trippet, S. E., & Bain, J. (1993). Physical health problems and concerns of lesbians. *Women and Health, 20*(2), 59-70.

34. White, J., & Martinez, M. C. (1997). *The lesbian health book: Caring for ourselves.* Seattle, WA: Seal Press.

HIV/AIDS Prevention with Gay & Bisexual Men

35. Diaz, R. M. (1998). *Latino gay men and HIV.* New York: Routledge.

   This book reviews and critiques the HIV prevention literature on Latino gay men, and explicates a model for understanding the sociocultural barriers to adopting or maintaining safer sex habits among them. It also describes a model HIV prevention program targeted to this population.

36. Doll, L. S., & Beeker, C. (1996). Male bisexual behavior and HIV risk in the United States: Synthesis of research with implications for behavioral interventions. *AIDS Education and Prevention, 8*(3), 205-225.

37. Martin, J. I., & Knox, J. (1995). HIV risk behavior in gay men with unstable self-esteem. *Journal of Gay & Lesbian Social Services, 2*(2), 21-41.

38. Martin, J. I., & Knox, J. (1997). Loneliness and sexual risk behavior in gay men. *Psychological Reports, 81,* 815-825.

39. Martin, J. I., & Knox, J. (1997). Self-esteem instability and its implications for HIV prevention among gay men. *Health & Social Work, 22,* 264-273.

   This article reports on a large survey of self-identified gay men that examined the relationships between self-esteem instability, unprotected anal intercourse, and other psychosocial variables. It discusses the implications of the findings for efforts to improve the effectiveness of HIV prevention efforts in this population.

40. McLean, J., Boulton, M., Brookes, M., Lakhani, D., Fitzpatrick, R., Dawson, J., McKechnie, R., & Hart, G. (1994). Regular partners and risky behaviour: Why do gay men have unprotected intercourse? *AIDS Care, 6,* 331-341.

41. Meyer, I. H., & Dean, L. (1998). Internalized homophobia, intimacy, and sexual behavior among gay and bisexual men. In G. M. Herek (Ed.), *Stigma and sexual orientation: Understanding prejudice against lesbians, gay men, and bisexuals* (pp. 160-186). Thousand Oaks, CA: Sage Publications.

42. Morales, J. (1995). Gay Latinos and AIDS: A framework for HIV/AIDS prevention curriculum. *Journal of Gay & Lesbian Social Services, 2*(3/4), 89-105.

43. Nieves-Rosa, L. E., Carballo-Dieguez, A., & Dolezal, C. (2000). Domestic abuse and HIV-risk behavior in Latin American men who have sex with men in New York City. *Journal of Gay & Lesbian Social Services, 11*(1), 77-90.

44. Odets, W. (1996). AIDS education and harm reduction for gay men: Psychological approaches for the 21st century. *AIDS & Public Policy Journal, 9*(1), 3-15.

This article examines themes of homophobia and moralizing in HIV prevention efforts among gay men. It critiques many prevention programs as destructive to gay men's psychosocial well-being, and presents guidelines for a new generation of efforts to prevent HIV in this population.

45. Remien, R. H., Carballo-Diéguez, A., & Wagner, G. (1995). Intimacy and sexual risk behaviour in serodiscordant male couples. *AIDS Care, 7*, 429-438.

46. Roffman, R. A., Beadnell, B., Ryan, R., & Downey, L. (1995). Telephone group counseling in reducing AIDS risk in gay and bisexual males. *Journal of Gay & Lesbian Social Services, 2*(3/4), 145-157.

This article describes an HIV prevention program targeted to gay and bisexual men that consists of group sessions conducted entirely by telephone. It includes a case study to illustrate the need for this program among men who are unable or unwilling to receive services in person.

47. Roffman, R. A., Picciano, J. F., Ryan, R., Beadnell, B., Fisher, D., Downey, L., & Kalichman, S. C. (1997). HIV-prevention group counseling delivered by telephone: An efficacy trial with gay and bisexual men. *AIDS and Behavior, 1*(2), 137-154.

48. Roffman, R. A., Picciano, J. F., Bolan, M., & Kalichman, S. C. (1997). Factors associated with attrition from an HIV-prevention program for gay and bisexual males. *AIDS and Behavior, 1*(2), 125-135.

49. Siebt, A. C., Ross, M. W., Freeman, A., Krepcho, M., Hedrich, A., McAlister, A., & Fernandez-Esquer, M. E. (1995). Relationship between safe sex and acculturation into the gay subculture. *AIDS Care, 7*, S85-S88.

50. Singer, M., & Marxuach-Rodriguez, L. (1996). Applying anthropology to the prevention of AIDS: The Latino Gay Men's Health Project. *Human Organization, 55*(2), 141-148.

51. Stokes, J. P., Vanable, P. A., & McKirnan, D. J. (1996). Ethnic differences in sexual behavior, condom use, and psychosocial variables among Black and White men who have sex with men. *Journal of Sex Research, 33*, 373-381.

52. Wright, M. T., Rosser, B. R., & de Zwart, O. (Eds.). (1998). *New international directions in HIV prevention for gay and bisexual men.* New York: Harrington Park Press.

This book contains a series of articles that critique the prevailing paradigm framing HIV prevention research and practice, especially in the U.S., and provide new models for understanding risky behaviors and for designing more effective prevention programs.

Gay & Bisexual Men Living with HIV/AIDS

53. Kadushin, G. (1999). Barriers to social support and support received from their families of origin among gay men with HIV/AIDS. *Health & Social Work, 24*, 198-209.

54. Kemeny, M. E., Weiner, H., Taylor, S. E., Schneider, S., Visscheer, B., & Fahey, J. L. (1994). Repeated bereavement, depressed mood, and immune parameters in HIV seropositive and seronegative gay men. *Health Psychology, 13*, 14-24.

55. Kimberly, J. A., & Serovich, J. M. (1999). The role of family and friend social support in reducing risk behaviors among HIV-positive gay men. *AIDS Education and Prevention, 11*, 465-475.

56.   Linsk, N. L. (1997). Experience of older gay and bisexual men living with HIV/AIDS. *Journal of Gay, Lesbian, and Bisexual Identity, 2,* 285-308.

57.   Mancoske, R. J. (1997). Rural HIV/AIDS social services for gays and lesbians. *Journal of Gay & Lesbian Social Services, 7*(3), 37-52.

   This article discusses the issues faced by gay and lesbian people living with HIV/AIDS in rural areas of the U.S., including the state of health care and social services available to them.

58.   Meyer, P., Tapley, E. K., & Bazargan, M. (1996). Depression in HIV symptomatic gay and bisexual men. *Journal of Gay & Lesbian Social Services, 5*(4), 69-85.

59.   Peterson, J. L., Folkman, S., & Bakeman, R. (1996). Stress, coping, HIV status, psychosocial resources, and depressive mood in African American gay, bisexual, and heterosexual men. *American Journal of Community Psychology, 24,* 461-487.

   This article reports on a study of coping among African American gay, bisexual, and heterosexual men, HIV negative and positive. Interview findings include an association between depression and physical health symptoms, and an association between stress and depression mediated by social support.

60.   Rodgers, A. Y. (1995). The relationship between changes in sexual support and adjustment to AIDS in gay males. *Social Work in Health Care, 20*(3), 37-49.

61.   Sandstrom, K. L. (1996). Searching for information, understanding, and self-value: The utilization of peer support groups by gay men with HIV/AIDS. *Social Work in Health Care, 23*(4), 51-74.

62.   Siegel, K., Karus, D., & Raveis, V. H. (1997). Correlates of change in depressive symptomatology among gay men with AIDS. *Health Psychology, 16,* 230-238.

Gay & Bisexual Men's Health Issues Other than HIV

63.   Lipton, B. (1997). Responding to non-HIV invisible chronic illness within the gay male community. *Journal of Gay & Lesbian Social Services, 7*(1), 93-98.

   This article discusses the impact of chronic illnesses other than HIV on gay men. It presents a case for expanding the scope of social services originally targeted to gay men living with AIDS in order to serve those living with other chronic conditions.

64.   Penn, R. E. (1997). *The gay men's wellness guide: The National Lesbian and Gay Health Association's complete book of physical, emotional, and mental health and well-being for every gay male.* New York: Henry Holt.

VI. Mental Health

1.   Alexander, C. J. (Ed.). (1996). *Gay and lesbian mental health: A sourcebook for practitioners.* New York: Harrington Park Press.

2.   Bailey, J. M. (1999). Homosexuality and mental illness. *Archives of General Psychiatry, 56,* 883-886.

3.   Bernhard, L. A., & Applegate, J. M. (1999). Comparison of stress and stress management strategies between lesbian and heterosexual women. *Health Care for Women International, 20,* 355-347.

4.   Bradford, J., Ryan, C., & Rothblum, E. D. (1994). National lesbian health care survey: Implications for mental health care. *Journal of Consulting and Clinical Psychology, 62,* 228-242.

5.   Cochran, S. D., & Mays, V. M. (1994). Depressive distress among homosexually active African American men and women. *American Journal of Psychiatry, 151,* 524-529.

6.   Cochran, S. D., & Mays, V. M. (2000). Relation between psychiatric syndromes and behaviorally defined sexual orientation in a sample of the U.S. Population. *American Journal of Epidemiology, 151,* 516-523.

This article reviews differences in 1-year prevalence rates of six psychiatric syndromes of sexually active persons who reported either exclusive heterosexuality or having any same-gender partners in the prior year.

7.   Cohen, L., de Ruiter, C., Ringelberg, H., & Cohen-Kettenis, P. T. (1997). Psychological functioning of adolescent transsexuals: Personality and psychopathology. *Journal of Clinical Psychology, 53,* 187-198.

8.   Descamps, M. J., Rothblum, E., Bradford, J., & Ryan, C. (2000). Mental health impact of child sexual abuse, rape, intimate partner violence, and hate crimes in the National Lesbian Health Care Survey. *Journal of Gay & Lesbian Social Services, 11*(1), 27-55.

9.   Frable, D. E., Wortman, C., & Joseph, J. (1997). Distress in a cohort of gay men: The importance of cultural stigma, personal visbility, community networks, and positive identity. *Journal of Personality, 65,* 599-624.

10.   Friedman, R. C. (1999). Homosexuality, psychopathology, and suicidality. *Archives of General Psychiatry, 56,* 887-888.

This article reviews a study on lifetime risk of suicidal behaviors among gay men.

11.   Greene, B. (1994). Ethnic minority lesbians and gay men: Mental health and treatment issues. *Journal of Consulting and Clinical Psychology, 62,* 243-251.

12.   Greene, B. (1994). Lesbian women of color: Triple jeopardy. In L. Comas-Diaz & B. Greene (Eds.), *Women of color* (pp. 389-427). New York: Guilford.

This chapter discusses cultural and mental health issues among lesbian women of color.

13.   Hughes, T. L., Haas, A. P., Razzano, L., Cassidy, R., & Mathews, A. (2000). Comparing lesbians' and heterosexual women's mental health: A multi-site survey. *Journal of Gay & Lesbian Social Services, 11*(1), 57-76.

14.   Hyman, B. (2000). The economic consequences of child sexual abuse for adult lesbian women. *Journal of Marriage and the Family, 62,* 199-211.

This article discusses the effects of child sexual abuse on the physical and mental health, educational attainment, and economic welfare of adult lesbians.

15. Klinger, R. L., & Stein, T. S. (1996). Impact of violence, childhood sexual abuse, and domestic violence and abuse on lesbians, bisexuals, and gay men. In R. P. Cabaj & T. S. Stein (Eds.), *Textbook of homosexuality and mental health* (pp. 801-817). Washington, DC: American Psychiatric Press.

16. Meyer, I. H. (1995). Minority stress and mental health in gay men. *Journal of Health and Social Behavior, 36,* 38-56.

   This article reports on the effects of internalized homophobia and other minority stressors on the mental health of 741 gay men in New York City.

17. Nakajima, G. A., Chan, Y. H., & Lee, K. (1996). Mental health issues for gay and lesbian Asian Americans. In R. P. Cabaj & T. S. Stein (Eds.), *Textbook of homosexuality and mental health* (pp. 563-581). Washington, DC: American Psychiatric Press.

18. Oetjen, H., & Rothblum, E. D. (2000). When lesbians aren't gay: Factors affecting depression among lesbians. *Journal of Homosexuality, 39*(1), 49-73.

19. Zea, M. C., Reisen, C. A., & Poppen, P. J. (1999). Psychological well-being among Latino lesbians and gay men. *Cultural Diversity & Ethnic Minority Psychology, 5,* 371-379.

   This article discusses factors associated with lower levels of depression and higher levels of personal self-esteem, such as active coping and social support.

VII. Alcohol and Drug Addiction

1. Abbott, L. J. (1998). The use of alcohol by lesbians: A review and research agenda. *Substance Use & Misuse, 33,* 2647-2663.

2. Anderson, S. C. (1996). Addressing heterosexist bias in the treatment of lesbian couples with chemical dependency. In J. Laird & R. J. Green (Eds.), *Lesbians and gays in couples and families* (pp. 316-340). San Francisco: Jossey-Bass.

3. Cabaj, R. P. (1995). Sexual orientation and the addictions. *Journal of Gay & Lesbian Psychotherapy, 2*(3), 97-117.

4. Cabaj, R. P. (1996). Substance abuse in gay men, lesbians, and bisexuals. In R. P. Cabaj & T. S. Stein (Eds.), *Textbook of homosexuality and mental health* (pp. 783-799). Washington, DC: American Psychiatric Press.

5. Finnegan, D. G., & McNally, E. B. (1996). Chemical dependency and depression in lesbians and gay men: What helps? *Journal of Gay & Lesbian Social Services, 4*(2), 115-129.

6. Hughes, T. L., & Wilsnack, S. C. (1997). Use of alcohol among lesbians: Research and clinical implications. *American Journal of Orthopsychiatry, 67,* 20-36.

   This article critically reviews the literature on alcohol use among lesbians, identifying methodological flaws in several studies.

7. Jordan, K. M. (2000). Substance abuse among gay, lesbian, bisexual, transgender, and questioning adolescents. *School Psychology Review, 29,* 201-206.

8. Kus, R. J., & Smith, G. B. (1995). Referrals and resources for chemically dependent gay and lesbian clients. *Journal of Gay & Lesbian Social Services, 2*(1), 91-107.

This article proposes that gay men and lesbians recovering from chemical dependency need different resources than other recovering persons.

9.   Parks, C. A. (1999). Bicultural competence: A mediating factor affecting alcohol use practices and problems among lesbian social drinkers. *Journal of Drug Issues, 29*, 135-154.

This article explores bicultural competence as a framework for viewing the diversity of drinking practices and consequences among lesbian social drinkers.

10.   Parks, C. A. (1999). Lesbian social drinking: The role of alcohol in growing up and living as lesbian. *Contemporary Drug Problems, 26*, 75-91.

11.   Reyes, M. (1998). Latina lesbians and alcohol and other drugs: Social work implications. *Alcoholism Treatment Quarterly, 16*, 179-192.

12.   Rosario, M., Hunter, J., & Gwadz, M. (1997). Exploration of substance use among lesbian, gay, and bisexual youth: Prevalence and correlates. *Journal of Adolescent Research, 12*, 454-476.

VIII. Intimate Partner Violence

1.   Bernhard, L. A. (2000). Physical and sexual violence experienced by lesbian and heterosexual women. *Violence Against Women, 6*, 68-79.

2.   Bograd, M. (1999). Strengthening domestic violence theories: Intersections of race, class, sexual orientation, and gender. *Journal of Marital and Family Therapy, 25*, 275-289.

3.   Burke, L. K., & Follingstad, D. R. (1999). Violence in lesbian and gay relationships: Theory, prevalence, and correlational factors. *Clinical Psychology Review, 19*, 487-512.

4.   Cruz, J. M., & Firestone, J. M. (1998). Exploring violence and abuse in gay male relationships. *Violence and Victims, 13*, 159-173.

This article reports qualitative data collected over 8 months with 25 gay men who self-identified as victims or perpetrators of domestic violence.

5.   Elliott, P. (1996). Shattering illusions: Same-sex domestic violence. *Journal of Gay & Lesbian Social Services, 4*(1), 1-8.

6.   Farley, N. (1996). A survey of factors contributing to gay and lesbian domestic violence. *Journal of Gay & Lesbian Social Services, 4*(1), 35-42.

7.   Girshick, L. B. (1999). Organizing in the lesbian community to confront lesbian battering. *Journal of Gay & Lesbian Social Services, 9*(1), 83-92.

8.   Hamberger, L. K. (1996). Intervention in gay male intimate violence calls for coordinated efforts on multiple levels. *Journal of Gay & Lesbian Social Services, 4*(1), 83-91.

9.   Istar, A. (1996). Couple assessment: Identifying and intervening in domestic violence in lesbian relationships. *Journal of Gay & Lesbian Social Services, 4*(1), 93-106.

10.   Klinger, R. L. (1995). Gay violence. *Journal of Gay & Lesbian Psychotherapy, 2*, 119-134.

11.   Landolt, M. A., & Dutton, D. G. (1997). Power and personality: An analysis of gay male intimate abuse. *Sex Roles, 37*, 335-359.

12.   Letellier, P. (1994). Gay and bisexual domestic violence victimization: Challenges to feminist theory and responses to violence. In L. K. Hamberger & C. Renzetti (Eds.), *Domestic partner abuse* (pp. 1-21). New York: Springer.

   This article discusses how same-sex male battering challenges contemporary feminist domestic violence theory.

13.   Letellier, P. (1996). Twin epidemics: Domestic violence and HIV infection among gay and bisexual men. *Journal of Gay and Lesbian Social Services, 4*(1), 69-81.

   This article discusses how HIV can be a weapon of control used to keep a gay man in a relationship with a violent partner.

14.   Leventhal, B., & Lundy, S. E. (Ed.). (1999). *Same-sex domestic violence: Strategies for change*. Thousand Oaks, CA: Sage Publications.

15.   Lockhart, L. L., White, B. A., Causby, B., & Isaac, A. (1994). Letting out the secret: Violence in lesbian relationships. *Journal of Interpersonal Violence, 9*, 469-492.

   This article examines the incidence, forms, and correlates of violence in lesbian relationships.

16.   Marrujo, B., & Kreger, M. (1996). Definitions of roles in abusive lesbian relationships. *Journal of Gay & Lesbian Social Services, 4*(1), 23-33.

17.   Mendez, J. M. (1996). Serving gays and lesbians of color who are survivors of domestic violence. *Journal of Gay & Lesbian Social Services, 4*(1), 53-59.

   This article addresses many topics concerning same-sex domestic violence, including legal issues, community and coalition-building, and services.

18.   Merrill, G. S. (1996). Ruling the exceptions: Same-sex battering and domestic violence theory. *Journal of Gay and Lesbian Social Services, 4*(1), 9-21.

   This article presents challenges to current gender-based domestic violence theory resulting from the existence of same-sex domestic violence.

19.   Renzetti, C. M. (1996). The poverty of services for battered lesbians. *Journal of Gay & Lesbian Social Services, 4*(1), 61-68.

   This article addresses the minimal number of services for lesbian victims of partner abuse, and the serious gap that exists between service providers' rhetoric and the reality of services provided.

20.   Scherzer, T. (1998). Domestic violence in lesbian relationships: Findings of the lesbian relationships research project. *Journal of Lesbian Studies, 2*, 29-47.

21.   Sloan, L., & Edmond, T. (1996). Shifting the focus: Recognizing the needs of lesbian and gay survivors of sexual violence. *Journal of Gay & Lesbian Social Services, 5*(4), 33-51.

22.   Tuel, B. D., & Russell, R. K. (1998). Self-esteem and depression in battered women: A comparison of lesbian and heterosexual survivors. *Violence Against Women, 4*, 344-362.

23.   Turell, S. C. (1999). Seeking help for same-sex relationship abuses. *Journal of Gay & Lesbian Social Services, 10*(2), 35-49.

24. Waldner-Haugrud, L. K. (1999). Sexual coercion in lesbian and gay relationships: A review and critique. *Aggression and Violent Behavior, 4,* 139-149.

    This article reviews and critiques several research studies on rates, causes, and effects of sexual coercion in lesbian and gay relationships.

25. Waldner-Haugrud, L. K., & Gratch, L. V. (1997). Sexual coercion in gay/lesbian relationships: Descriptives and gender differences. *Violence and Victims, 12,* 87-98.

26. Waldner-Haugrud, L. K., Gratch, L. V., & Magruder, B. (1997). Victimization and perpetration rates of violence in gay and lesbian relationships: Gender issues explored. *Violence and Victims, 12,* 173-184.

27. Waldron, C. M. (1996). Lesbians of color and the domestic violence movement. *Journal of Gay & Lesbian Social Services, 4*(1), 43-59.

    This article discusses the effects of racism and heterosexism on lesbians of color in roles as survivor, batterer, and service provider.

IX. Practice Issues

General Practice Issues

1. Cabaj, R. P. (1996). Sexual orientation of the therapist. In R. P. Cabaj & T. S. Stein (Eds.), *Textbook of homosexuality and mental health* (pp. 513-524). Washington, DC: American Psychiatric Press.

2. Fassinger, R. E. (2000). Applying counseling theories to lesbian, gay, and bisexual clients: Pitfalls and possibilities. In R. M. Perez & K. A. DeBord (Eds.), *Handbook of counseling and psychotherapy with lesbian, gay, and bisexual clients* (pp. 107-131). Washington, DC: American Psychological Association.

    This chapter summarizes the core aspects of humanistic, cognitive-behavioral, psychodynamic, and systems-cultural approaches in counseling, and discusses the potential advantages and hazards of using each of them with lesbian, gay, or bisexual clients.

3. Foster, S. J. (1997). Rural lesbians and gays: Public perceptions, worker perceptions, and service delivery. *Journal of Gay & Lesbian Social Services, 7*(3), 23-35.

4. Greene, B. (1997). Ethnic minority lesbians and gay men: Mental health and treatment issues. In B. Greene (Ed.), *Ethnic and cultural diversity among lesbians and gay men* (pp. 216-239). Thousand Oaks, CA: Sage Publications.

5. Haldeman, D. C. (1994). The practice and ethics of sexual orientation conversion therapy. *Journal of Consulting and Clinical Psychology, 62,* 221-227.

    This article reviews the empirical literature on efforts to change gay men's and lesbians' sexual orientation, and it discusses the ethical implications of sexual orientation conversion therapy.

6. Hartman, A., & Laird, J. (1998). Moral and ethical issues in working with lesbians and gay men. *Families in Society, 79,* 263-276.

7.   Hess, P. M., & Hess, H. J. (1998). Values and ethics in social work practice with lesbian and gay persons. In G. P. Mallon (Ed.), *Foundations of social work practice with lesbian and gay persons* (pp. 31-46). New York: Harrington Park Press.

This book chapter explains how the core values and ethical principles of social work, as defined by the NASW Code of Ethics, apply to practice with lesbian and gay clients. It uses case examples to illustrate the application of these principles.

8.   Jones, M. A., & Gabriel, M. A. (1999). Utilization of psychotherapy by lesbians, gay men, and bisexuals: Findings from a nationwide survey. *American Journal of Orthopsychiatry, 69,* 209-219.

This article reports on a survey of the experiences with psychotherapy in a large nationwide sample of lesbians, gay men, and bisexuals. It focuses on patterns of psychotherapy use and differences in experience according to the sexual orientation of the therapist.

9.   Lebolt, J. (1999). Gay affirmative psychotherapy: A phenomenological study. *Clinical Social Work Journal, 27,* 355-370.

10.   Levy, E. F. (1995). Feminist social work practice with lesbian and gay clients. In Van Den Bergh, N. (Ed.), *Feminist practice in the 21st century* (pp. 278-294). Washington, DC: National Association of Social Workers.

11.   Martin, J. I. (1997). Political aspects of mental health treatment. In T. R. Watkins & J. W. Callicutt (Eds.), *Mental health policy and practice today* (pp.32-48). Thousand Oaks, CA: Sage Publications.

This book chapter discusses how psychiatric diagnosis and psychotherapeutic treatment of lesbians and gay men always exists within a sociopolitical context, and draws parallels between the oppressive treatment of lesbians, gay men, women, and ethnic minorities.

12.   Murphy, T. F. (1992). Redirecting sexual orientation: Techniques and justifications. *The Journal of Sex Research, 29,* 501-523.

13.   National Association of Social Workers. (2000). *"Reparative" and "conversion" therapies for lesbians and gay men* [Brochure]. Washington, DC: Author.

14.   Sorensen, L., & Roberts, S. J. (1997). Lesbian uses of and satisfaction with mental health services: Results from a Boston lesbian health project. *Journal of Homosexuality, 33*(1), 35-49.

15.   Tully, C. T. (2000). *Lesbians, gays, and the empowerment perspective.* New York: Columbia University Press.

Practice with Individuals

16.   Abramowitz, S., & Cohen, J. (1994). The psychodynamics of AIDS: A view from self psychology. In S. A. Cadwell, R. A. Burnham, & M. Forstein (Eds.), *Therapists on the front line: Psychotherapy with gay men in the age of AIDS* (pp. 205-221). Washington, DC: American Psychiatric Press.

This chapter uses self psychology theory and case examples to describe the subjective experience of some gay men living with AIDS, focusing on the ways in which AIDS may disrupt their self-cohesiveness. It provides guidelines for conducting clinical work with this population, and explains some likely effects of doing so on the self of the clinician.

17. Cadwell, S. A. (1994). Empathic challenges for gay male therapists working with HIV-infected gay men. In S. A. Cadwell, R. A. Burnham, & M. Forstein (Eds.), *Therapists on the front line: Psychotherapy with gay men in the age of AIDS* (pp. 475-496). Washington, DC: American Psychiatric Press.

18. Chan, C. S. (1992). Cultural considerations in counseling Asian American lesbians and gay men. In S. H. Dworkin & F. J. Gutierrez (Eds.), *Counseling gay men & lesbians: Journey to the end of the rainbow* (pp. 115-124). Alexandria, VA: American Association for Counseling and Development.

19. Cohler, B. J., & Galatzer-Levy, R. (1996). Self psychology and homosexuality. In R. P. Cabaj & T. S. Stein (Eds.), *Textbook of homosexuality and mental health* (pp. 207-223). Washington, DC: American Psychiatric Press.

20. Gabriel, M. A., & Monaco, G. W. (1995). Revisiting the question of self-disclosure: The lesbian therapist's dilemma. In J. M. Glassgold & S. Iasenza (Eds.), *Lesbians and psychoanalysis: Revolutions in theory and practice* (pp. 161-172). New York: Free Press.

21. Gartrell, N. K. (1992). Boundaries in lesbian therapist-client relationships. *Women & Therapy, 12*(3), 29-50.

22. Goldstein, E. (1997). Clinical practice with lesbians. In J. R. Brandell (Ed.), *Theory and practice in clinical social work* (pp. 599-617). New York: Free Press.

23. Greene, B. (1995). Addressing racism, sexism, and heterosexism in psychoanalytic psychotherapy. In J. M. Glassgold, & S. Iasenza (Eds.), *Lesbians and psychoanalysis: Revolutions in theory and practice* (pp. 145-159). New York: Free Press.

24. Gutierrez, F. J., & Dworkin, S. H. (1992). Gay, lesbian, and African American: Managing the integration of identities. In S. H. Dworkin & F. J. Gutierrez (Eds.), *Counseling gay men & lesbians: Journey to the end of the rainbow* (pp. 141-156). Alexandria, VA: American Association for Counseling and Development.

25. Hellman, R. E. (1996). Issues in the treatment of lesbian women and gay men with chronic mental illness. *Psychiatric Services, 47,* 1093-1098.

This article describes some concerns of lesbians and gay men with chronic mental illnesses, and it provides guidelines for affirmative treatment with this population in both inpatient and outpatient settings.

26. Icard, L. D. (1996). Assessing the psychosocial well-being of African American gays: A multidimensional perspective. *Journal of Gay & Lesbian Social Services, 5*(2/3), 25-49.

27. Lesser, J. G. (1999). When your son becomes your daughter: A mother's adjustment to a transgender child. *Families in Society, 80,* 182-189.

This article describes the case of a depressed woman whose son had sex reassignment surgery and became her daughter. It provides a description of individual treatment of the woman based on self psychology, including the reactions of the social worker.

28. Mallon, G. P. (1994). Counseling strategies with gay and lesbian youth. *Journal of Gay & Lesbian Social Services, 1*(3/4), 75-91.

29. Mallon, G. P. (1999). Practice with transgendered children. *Journal of Gay & Lesbian Social Services, 10*(3/4), 49-64.

30. Matteson, D. R. (1996). Psychotherapy with bisexual individuals. In R. P. Cabaj & T. S. Stein (Eds.), *Textbook of homosexuality and mental health* (pp. 433-450). Washington, DC: American Psychiatric Press.

31. Morales, E. S. (1992). Counseling Latino gays and Latina lesbians. In S. H. Dworkin & F. J. Gutierrez (Eds.), *Counseling gay men & lesbians: Journey to the end of rainbow* (pp. 125-139). Alexandria, VA: American Association for Counseling and Development.

32. Mylott, K. (1994). Twelve irrational ideas that drive gay men and women crazy. *Journal of Rational-Emotive & Cognitive-Behavior Therapy, 12*(1), 61-71.

   This article uses a Rational Emotive Behavior Therapy (REBT) model to explain how irrational ideas may underlie emotional disturbances among lesbians or gay men. Although it does not directly provide treatment guidelines, the article might be especially helpful to those familiar with REBT attempting to adapt the model for work with gay and lesbian clients.

33. Paradis, B. A. (1993). A self psychological approach to the treatment of gay men with AIDS. *Clinical Social Work Journal, 21,* 405-416.

34. Stein, T. S., & Cabaj, R. P. (1996). Psychotherapy with gay men. In R. P. Cabaj & T. S. Stein (Eds.), *Textbook of homosexuality and mental health* (pp. 413-432). Washington, DC: American Psychiatric Press.

35. Steinhorn, A. I. (1998). Individual practice with lesbians. In G. P. Mallon (Ed.), *Foundations of social work practice with lesbians and gay persons* (pp. 105-129). New York: Harrington Park Press.

36. Swann, S., & Herbert, S. E. (1999). Ethical issues in the mental health treatment of gender dysphoric adolescents. *Journal of Gay & Lesbian Social Services, 10*(3/4), 19-34.

37. Thompson, B. J. (1994). Home to die: Therapy with HIV-infected gay men in smaller urban areas. In Cadwell, S. A., Burnham, R. A., & Forstein, M. (Eds.), *Therapists on the front line: Psychotherapy with gay men in the age of AIDS* (pp. 275-291). Washington, DC: American Psychiatric Press.

Practice with Couples

38. Anderson, S. C. (1996). Addressing heterosexist bias in the treatment of lesbian couples with chemical dependency. In J. Laird & R. J. Green (Eds.), *Lesbians and gays in couples and families* (pp. 316-340). San Francisco: Jossey-Bass.

39. Burke, J. L., & Faber, P. (1997). A genogrid for couples. *Journal of Gay & Lesbian Social Services, 7*(1), 13-22.

   This article explains how to use a genogrid in assessments of lesbian and gay couples in clinical practice.

40. Byrne, D. (1996). Clinical models for the treatment of gay male perpetrators of domestic violence. *The Journal of Gay & Lesbian Services, 4*(1), 107-116.

   This article discusses the role of internalized homophobia among gay men who act abusively toward their partners. It presents several intervention models.

41. Deacon, S. A., Reinke, L., & Viers, D. (1996). Cognitive-behavioral therapy for bisexual couples: Expanding the realms of therapy. *American Journal of Family Therapy, 24,* 242-250.

42. Falco, K. (1991). *Psychotherapy with lesbian clients: Theory into practice.* New York: Brunner/Mazel.

43. Fisher, S. K. (1993). A proposed Adlerian theoretical framework and intervention techniques for gay and lesbian couples. *Individual Psychology, 49,* 438-449.

44. Gray, D., & Isensee, R. (1996). Balancing autonomy and intimacy in lesbian and gay relationships. In C. J. Alexander (Ed.), *Gay and lesbian mental health: A sourcebook for practitioners* (pp. 95-114). New York: Harrington Park Press.

45. Greene, B., & Boyd-Franklin, N. (1996). African American lesbians: Issues in couples therapy. In J. Laird & R. J. Green (Eds.), *Lesbians and gays in couples and families* (pp. 251-271). San Francisco: Jossey-Bass.

46. Kerewsky, S. D., & Miller, D. (1996). Lesbian couples and childhood trauma: Guidelines for therapists. In J. Laird & R. J. Green (Eds.), *Lesbians and gays in couples and families* (pp. 298-315). San Francisco: Jossey-Bass.

   This book chapter explains several ways in which childhood trauma among lesbians might impact their adult intimate relationships. It describes a model for clinical practice with lesbian couples impacted by the sequelae of childhood trauma.

47. Laird, J. (1994). Lesbian families: A cultural perspective. *Smith College Studies in Social Work, 64,* 263-296.

48. LaSala, M. C. (1998). Coupled gay men, parents, and in-laws: Intergenerational disapproval and the need for a thick skin. *Families in Society, 79,* 585-595.

   This article reports on interviews with coupled gay men concerning their relationships with in-laws, focusing on boundary-setting strategies employed to cope with in-law hostility. It provides guidelines for clinical practice with gay couples experiencing intergenerational stress.

49. Levy, E. F. (1992). Strengthening the coping resources of lesbian families. *Families in Society, 73,* 23-31.

50. McClennen, J. C., & Gunther, J. (1999). *A professional's guide to understanding gay and lesbian domestic violence: Understanding practice interventions.* Lewiston, NY: Edwin Mellen.

51. McVinney, L. D. (1998). Social work practice with gay male couples. In G. P. Mallon (Ed.), *Foundations of social work practice with lesbians and gay persons* (pp. 209-227). New York: Harrington Park Press.

52. Ramirez Barranti, C. C. (1998). Social work practice with lesbian couples. In G. P. Mallon (Ed.), *Foundations of social work practice with lesbians and gay persons* (pp. 183-207). New York: Harrington Park Press.

53. Slater, S. (1994). Approaching and avoiding the work of the middle years: Affairs in committed lesbian relationships. *Women & Therapy, 15*(2), 19-34.

54. Sussal, C. M. (1993). Object relations couples therapy with lesbians. *Smith College Studies in Social Work, 63,* 301-317.

This article explains central concepts of object relations couples therapy and illustrates with extensive case examples how they may be applied in clinical work with lesbian couples.

55. Wise, A. J., & Bowman, S. L. (1997). Comparisons of beginning counselors' responses to lesbian vs. heterosexual partner abuse. *Violence and Victims, 12,* 127-135.

Practice with Families

56. Bigner, J. J. (1996). Working with gay fathers: Developmental, postdivorce parenting, and therapeutic issues. In J. Laird & R. J. Green (Eds.), *Lesbians and gays in couples and families* (pp. 370-403). San Francisco: Jossey-Bass.

57. Bryant, S. (1992). Mediation for lesbian and gay families. *Mediation Quarterly, 9,* 391-395.

58. Emerson, S., & Rosenfeld, C. (1996). Stages of adjustment in family members of transgender individuals. *Journal of Family Psychotherapy, 7*(3), 1-12.

59. Faria, G. (1994). Training for family preservation practice with lesbian families. *Families in Society, 75,* 416-422.

60. Granvold, D. K., & Martin, J. I. (1999). Family therapy with gay and lesbian clients. In C. Franklin & C. Jordan (Eds.), *Family practice: Brief systems methods for social work* (pp. 299-320). Pacific Grove, CA: Brooks/Cole.

This book chapter summarizes unique characteristics of lesbian and gay families, and it includes a case example that illustrates a cognitive-behavioral intervention strategy with a gay couple.

61. Laird, J. (1996). Family-centered practice with lesbian and gay families. *Families in Society, 77,* 559-572.

This article reviews and critiques research literature on lesbian and gay families, and uses a detailed case example to illustrate how constructionist and narrative approaches may be used in family therapy with lesbian and gay clients.

62. Laird, J. (1995). Family-centered practice: Feminist, constructionist, and cultural perspectives. In Van Den Bergh, N. (Ed.), *Feminist practice in the 21st century* (pp. 20-40). Washington, DC: National Association of Social Workers.

63. LaSala, M. C. (2000). Lesbians, gay men, and their parents: Family therapy for the coming-out crisis. *Family Process, 39,* 67-81.

64. Long, J. K. (1996). Working with lesbians, gays, and bisexuals: Addressing heterosexism in supervision. *Family Processes, 35,* 377-388.

65. Mallon, G. P. (1998). Social work practice with gay men and lesbians within families. In G. P. Mallon (Ed.), *Foundations of social work practice with lesbians and gay persons* (pp. 145-181). New York: Harrington Park Press.

This book chapter uses numerous case examples to illustrate an ecological understanding of gay men and lesbians within the context of families, and it provides specific guidelines for clinical intervention.

66. Mallon, G. P. (1999). *Let's get this straight: A gay- and lesbian-affirming approach to child welfare.* New York: Columbia University Press.

67. Rosenfeld, C., & Emerson, S. (1998). A process model of supportive therapy for families of transgender individuals. In D. Denny (Ed.), *Current concepts of transgendered identity* (pp. 391-400). New York: Garland.

68. Shuster, S. (1996). Families coping with HIV disease in gay fathers: Dimensions of treatment. In J. Laird & R. J. Green (Eds.), *Lesbians and gays in couples and families* (pp. 404-437). San Francisco: Jossey-Bass.

69. Zamarripa, M. X. (1997). A social constructionist approach for working with ethnic minority gay men and lesbians. *Family Therapy, 24,* 167-176.

This article uses a detailed case example in order to illustrate how the use of social constructionist approaches in family therapy may be particularly helpful in clinical work with ethnic minority lesbian and gay clients.

Practice with Groups

70. Ball, S. (1994). A group model for gay and lesbian clients with chronic mental illness. *Social Work, 39,* 109-115.

This article describes a model group for gay men and lesbians with chronic mental illnesses, including steps taken to overcome institutional resistance to it. It includes a detailed case example to illustrate the group's process and development, as well as the leader's intervention strategies.

71. Ball, S. (1998). A time limited group model for HIV-negative gay men. *Journal of Gay & Lesbian Social Services, 8*(1), 23-41.

72. Ball, S., & Lipton, B. (1997). Group work with gay men. In G. L. Greif & P. H. Ephross (Eds.), *Group work with populations at risk* (pp. 259-277). New York: Oxford University Press.

73. Christian, D. V., & Keefe, D. A. (1997). Maturing gay men: A framework for social service assessment and intervention. *Journal of Gay & Lesbian Social Services, 6*(1), 47-78.

74. Cramer, E. P., & Eldridge, T. L. (1997). Les Ms.: Creating an education and support group for lesbians. *Journal of Gay & Lesbian Social Services, 7*(1), 49-72.

This article describes in detail the planning, implementation, and evaluation of an education and support group for women who are lesbian, bisexual, or questioning their sexual orientation. It provides recommendations for similar groups with this population.

75. DeBord, K. A., & Perez, R. M. (2000). Group counseling theory and practice with lesbian, gay, and bisexual clients. In R. M. Perez & K. A. DeBord (Eds.), *Handbook of counseling and psychotherapy with lesbian, gay, and bisexual clients* (pp. 183-206). Washington, DC: American Psychological Association.

This book chapter explains how important therapeutic factors in group therapy apply to clinical work with lesbians, bisexuals, and gay men. It provides numerous suggestions for ways in which group therapists can promote positive change and growth in group work with members of these populations.

76. De Vidas, M. (1999). Childhood sexual abuse and domestic violence: A support group for Latino gay men and lesbians. *Journal of Gay & Lesbian Social Services, 10*(2), 51-68.

77. Engelhardt, B. J. (1997). Group work with lesbians. In G. L. Greif & P. H. Ephross (Eds.), *Group work with populations at risk* (pp. 278-291). New York: Oxford University Press.

78. Fassinger, R. E. (1997). Issues in group work with older lesbians. *Group, 21,* 191-210.

79. Foster, S. B., Stevens, P. E., & Hall, J. M. (1994). Offering support group services for lesbians living with HIV. *Women & Therapy, 15*(2), 69-83.

80. Getzel, G. S. (1998). Group work practice with gay men and lesbians. In G. P. Mallon (Ed.), *Foundations of social work practice with lesbians and gay persons* (pp. 131-144). New York: Harrington Park Press.

81. Glassman, N. S., & Frederick, R. J. (1998). When seronegative gay male therapists work with seronegative gay male clients: Countertransference issues in time-limited group psychotherapy. *Journal of Gay & Lesbian Social Services, 8*(1), 43-59.

82. Helfand, K. L. (1993). Therapeutic considerations in structuring a support group for the mentally ill gay/lesbian population. *Journal of Gay & Lesbian Psychotherapy, 2*(1), 65-76.

83. Klein, R. (1999). Group work with transgendered male to female sex workers. *Journal of Gay & Lesbian Social Services, 10*(3/4), 95-109.

This article describes a group for transgender adolescents who engage in sex work. It explains the role of sex work in their lives, and provides guidelines for group work practice with this population.

84. Koetting, M. E. (1996). A group design for HIV-negative gay men. *Social Work, 41,* 407-415.

85. Kus, R. J., & Latcovich, M. A. (1995). Special interest groups in Alcoholics Anonymous: A focus on gay men's groups. *Journal of Gay and Lesbian Social Services, 2*(1), 67-82.

86. Lipton, B. (1996). Opening doors: Responding to the mental health needs of gay and bisexual college students. *Journal of Gay & Lesbian Social Services, 4*(2), 7-24.

This article describes a group for gay and bisexual college students led by a graduate social work intern. It explains the need for this group in the context of student counseling services on a large urban campus, and provides guidelines for running similar groups elsewhere.

87. Morrow, D. F. (1996). Coming-out issues for adult lesbians: A group intervention. *Social Work, 41,* 647-656.

88. O'Donnell, J., Ferreira, J., & Malin, M. (1997). Collaboration between youth and adults in a support group for gay and lesbian youth. *Journal of Gay & Lesbian Social Services, 6*(3), 77-81.

89. Sandstrom, K. L. (1996). Searching for information, understanding, and self-value: The utilization of peer support groups by gay men with HIV/AIDS. *Social Work in Health Care, 23*(4), 51-74.

90. Saulnier, C. F. (1997). Alcohol problems and marginalization: Social group work with lesbians. *Social Work with Groups, 20,* 37-59.

    This article discusses the use of social group work with lesbians who are experiencing problems with alcohol.

91. Slusher, M. P., Mayer, C. J., & Dunkle, R. E. (1996). Gays and lesbians older and wiser (GLOW): A support group for older people. *The Gerontologist, 36,* 118-123.

92. Tunnell, G. (1994). Special issues in group psychotherapy for gay men with AIDS. In S. A. Cadwell, R. A. Burnham, & M. Forstein (Eds.), *Therapists on the front line: Psychotherapy with gay men in the age of AIDS* (pp. 237-254). Washington, DC: American Psychiatric Press.

Practice with Organizations & Communities

93. Appleby, G. A. (1998). Social work practice with gay men and lesbians within organizations. In G. P. Mallon (Ed.), *Foundations of social work practice with lesbians and gay persons* (pp. 249-269). New York: Harrington Park Press.

94. Beeler, J. A., Rawls, T. W., Herdt, G., & Cohler, B. J. (1999). The needs of older lesbians and gay men in Chicago. *Journal of Gay & Lesbian Social Services, 9*(1), 31-49.

95. Dworkin, J., & Kaufer, D. (1995). Social services and bereavement in the lesbian and gay community. *Journal of Gay & Lesbian Social Services, 2*(3/4), 41-60.

96. Fontaine, J. H. (1997). The sound of silence: Public school response to the needs of gay and lesbian youth. *Journal of Gay & Lesbian Social Services, 7*(4), 101-109.

97. Garnets, L. D., & D'Augelli, A. R. (1994). Empowering lesbian and gay communities: A call for collaboration with community psychology. *American Journal of Community Psychology, 22,* 447-470.

    This article describes past and present empowerment efforts undertaken by lesbian and gay communities. Although it is written for a community psychology readership, it identifies many needs for macro intervention among contemporary lesbian and gay communities.

98. Greeley, G. (1994). Service organizations for gay and lesbian youth. *Journal of Gay & Lesbian Social Services, 1*(3/4), 111-130.

99. Hidalgo, H. (1995). The norms of conduct in social service agencies: A threat to the mental health of Puerto Rican lesbians. *Journal of Gay & Lesbian Social Services, 3*(2), 23-41.

100. Hunter, J., & Mallon, G. P. (1998). Social work practice with gay men and lesbians within communities. In G. P. Mallon (Ed.), *Foundations of social work practice with lesbians and gay persons* (pp. 229-248). New York: Harrington Park Press.

101. Mallon, G.P. (1997). Entering a collaborative search for meaning with gay and lesbian youth in out-of-home care: An empowerment-based model for training child welfare professionals. *Child and Adolescent Social Work Journal, 14,* 427-444.

102. Mallon, G. P. (1999). A call for organizational trans-formation. *Journal of Gay & Lesbian Social Services, 10*(3/4), 131-142.

103. Mallon, G. P. (1999). *Let's get this straight: A gay- and lesbian-affirming approach to child welfare.* New York: Columbia University Press.

> **This book examines child welfare practice with gay and lesbian children and adolescents. It includes numerous case examples to describe the experiences of youths in the child welfare system. The book also critiques current child welfare practices and policies and describes a model of affirmative child welfare practice.**

104. Mann, W. M. (1997). Portraits of social services programs for rural sexual minorities. *Journal of Gay & Lesbian Social Services, 7*(3), 95-103.

105. Metz, P. (1997). Staff development for working with lesbian and gay elders. *Journal of Gay & Lesbian Social Services, 6*(1), 35-45.

106. Phillips, S., McMillen, C., Sparks, J., & Ueberle, M. (1997). Concrete strategies for sensitizing youth-serving agencies to the needs of gay, lesbian, and other sexual minority youths. *Child Welfare, 77,* 393-409.

107. Poverny, L. M. (2000). Employee assistance practice with sexual minorities. *Administration in Social Work, 23,* 69-91.

> **This article addresses employee assistance practice with lesbian and gay workers including strategies to use with workers, managers, and policy makers in the workplace.**

108. Powers, B. (1996). The effect of gay, lesbian, and bisexual workplace issues on productivity. *Journal of Gay & Lesbian Social Services, 4,* 79-90.

109. Schreier, B. A., & Werden, D. L. (2000). Psychoeducational programming: Creating a context of mental health for people who are lesbian, gay, or bisexual. In R. M. Perez & K. A. DeBord (Eds.), *Handbook of counseling and psychotherapy with lesbian, gay, and bisexual clients* (pp. 359-382). Washington, DC: American Psychological Association.

> **This book chapter discusses ways in which mental health services can be expanded to better serve the needs of lesbian, gay, and bisexual people. It describes some exercises that can be used to help sensitize staff, and includes guidelines for marketing and evaluating services.**

110. Smith, J. D. (1997). Working with larger systems: Rural lesbians and gays. *Journal of Gay & Lesbian Social Services, 7*(3), 13-21.

111. Sullivan, T. R. (1994). Obstacles to effective child welfare service with gay and lesbian youth. *Child Welfare, 73,* 291-304.

112. Uribe, V., & Harbeck, K. M. (1992). Addressing the needs of lesbian, gay, and bisexual youth: The origins of PROJECT 10 and school-based intervention. *Journal of Homosexuality, 22*(3/4), 9-28.

113. Wilson, P. A. (1995). AIDS service organizations: Current issues and future challenges. *Journal of Gay & Lesbian Social Services, 2*(3/4), 121-144.

> **This article describes the development, varieties of structure, and challenges of AIDS service organizations as new contexts for helping people living with HIV/AIDS.**

114. Yoakam, J. R. (1999). The Youth and AIDS Projects: School and community outreach for gay, lesbian, bisexual, and transgender youth. *Journal of Gay & Lesbian Social Services, 9*(4), 99-114.

This article describes how a network of 45 support groups for lesbian, gay, bisexual, and transgender youth in Minnesota schools was developed. It illustrates a variety of strategies needed to implement and expand this model program.

X. Policy Issues

1. Antoniuk, T. (1999). Policy alternatives for a diverse community: Lesbians and family law. *Journal of Gay & Lesbian Social Services, 10*(1), 47-60.

2. Badgett, M. V. (1994). Equal pay for equal families. *Academe, 80,* 26-30.

   This article stresses the need for unmarried heterosexual and same-sex couples to join together in advocating for domestic partner benefits.

3. Crawford, J. M. (1999). Co-parent adoptions by same-sex couples: From loophole to law. *Families in Society, 80,* 271-278.

4. Currah, P., Minter, S., & Green, J. (2000). *Transgender equality: A handbook for activitists and policymakers.* New York: National Gay & Lesbian Task Force Policy Institute.

5. Feilly, T. (1996). Gay and lesbian adoptions: A theoretical examination of policy-making and organizational decision making. *Journal of Sociology and Social Welfare, 23,* 99-115.

6. Gant, L. M. (2000). Identifying and confronting racism in AIDS service organizations. In M. Shernoff (Ed.), *AIDS and mental health practice* (pp. 309-318). New York: Haworth Press.

7. Gilmore, A. (1996). Employment protection for lesbians and gay men. *Law & Sexuality, 6,* 83-108.

   This article explores the legal claims gay and lesbian persons can use in challenging employment discrimination on grounds of sexual orientation.

8. Hartman, A. (1996). Social policy as a context for lesbian and gay families: The political is personal. In J. Laird & R. J. Green (Eds.), *Lesbians and gays in couples and families* (pp. 69-85). San Francisco: Jossey-Bass.

   This book chapter explains how several areas of U.S. social policy impact the family relationships of lesbians and gay men. It includes attention to civil rights, criminalization of same-sex sexual contact, and policies regarding lesbian and gay-headed families.

9. Mallon, G. P. (1998). *We don't exactly get the welcome wagon.* New York: Columbia University Press.

10. Mallon, G. P. (1999). *Let's get this straight: A gay- and lesbian-affirming approach to child welfare.* New York: Columbia University Press.

11. Patterson, C. J., & Redding, R. E. (1996). Lesbian and gay families with children: Implications of social science research for policy. *Journal of Social Issues, 52*(3), 29-50.

This article describes the various ways in which family law is applied to lesbian and gay parents and their children across jurisdictions in the U.S., and it explains how social science research supports the rights of members of this population. It suggests ways in which researchers can contribute to the development of nondiscriminatory family policy.

12. Poverny, L. (1999). It's all a matter of attitude: Creating and maintaining receptive services for sexual minority families. *Journal of Gay & Lesbian Social Services, 10*(1), 95-113.

13. Sartorelli, J. (1994). Gay rights and affirmative action. *Journal of Homosexuality, 27*(3/4), 179-232.

This article argues that many conditions that justify current affirmative action programs might also apply to lesbian and gay persons.

14. Sullivan, A. (Ed.). (1994). *Issues in gay and lesbian adoption: Proceedings of the Fourth Annual Pierce-Warwick Adoption Symposium.* Washington, DC: Child Welfare League of America.

This volume focuses on policy, legal, and research issues related to gay and lesbian adoptions of children.

15. Sullivan, T. R. (1994). Obstacles to effective child welfare service with gay and lesbian youths. *Child Welfare, 73,* 291-304.

16. Sullivan, T. R., & Baques, A. (1999). Familism and the adoption choice for gay and lesbian parents. *Journal of Gay & Lesbian Social Services, 10*(1), 79-94.

This article explores changing practices in adoption for lesbian and gay persons in both legal and political contexts.

17. Swan, W. K. (Ed.). (1997). *Gay/lesbian/bisexual/transgender public policy issues: A citizen's and administrator's guide to the new cultural struggle.* New York: Harrington Park Press.

This book examines a variety of U.S. public policy issues that affect lesbians, gay men, bisexuals, and transgender people. It includes policies involving the workplace, public education, families, sexual behavior, and hate violence.

18. Taylor, N. (1994). Gay and lesbian youth: Challenging the policy of denial. *Journal of Gay & Lesbian Social Services, 1*(3/4), 39-73.

19. Vaid, U. (1995). *Virtual equality.* New York: Anchor Books.

XI. Research Issues

20. Bieschke, K. J., McClanahan, M., Tozer, E., Grzegorek, J. L., & Park, J. (2000). Programmatic research on the treatment of lesbian, gay, and bisexual clients: The past, the present, and the course for the future. In R. M. Perez & K. A. DeBord (Eds.), *Handbook of counseling and psychotherapy with lesbian, gay, and bisexual clients* (pp. 309-335). Washington, DC: American Psychological Association.

This book chapter reviews and critiques the methodology of research on psychotherapeutic treatment of lesbian, gay, and bisexual clients. It provides numerous recommendations for future research, with emphasis on strategies to improve upon the methodological limitations of previous studies.

21. Brady, S., & Busse, W. J. (1994). The Gay Identity Questionnaire: A brief measure of homosexual identity formation. *Journal of Homosexuality, 26*(4), 1-22.

22. Dunkle, J. H. (1994). Counseling gay male clients: A review of treatment efficacy research: 1975-present. *Journal of Gay & Lesbian Psychotherapy, 2*(2), 1-19.

23. Hooker, E. (1993). Reflections of a 40-year exploration: A scientific view on homosexuality. *American Psychologist, 48*, 450-453.

24. Icard, L. D., Longres, J. F., & Williams, J. H. (1996). An applied research agenda for homosexually active men of color. *Journal of Gay & Lesbian Social Services, 5*(2/3), 139-164.

25. Kadushin, G. (1997). Researching a sensitive topic: Designing a mail survey of the perceptions of gay men with HIV/AIDS regarding social support received from the family of origin. *Social Work in Health Care, 25*(4), 1-11.

26. Laird, J. (1996). Family-centered practice with lesbian and gay families. *Families in Society, 77*, 559-572.

27. Martin, J. I., & Knox, J. (2000). Methodological and ethical issues in research on lesbians and gay men. *Social Work Research, 24*, 51-59.

This article describes several issues likely to impact studies of lesbians and gay men. These include theory and problem formulation issues, difficulties with defining the population of interest, sampling challenges, and strategies to prevent harm to participants.

28. Morris, J. F., & Rothblum, E. D. (1999). Who fills out a "lesbian" questionnaire?: The interrelationship of sexual orientation, years "out," disclosure of sexual orientation, sexual experience with women, and participation in the lesbian community. *Psychology of Women Quarterly, 23*, 537-557.

29. Roffman, R. A., Picciano, J., Wickizer, L., Bolan, M., & Ryan, R. (1998). Anonymous enrollment in AIDS prevention telephone group counseling: Facilitating the participation of gay and bisexual men in intervention and research. *Journal of Social Service Research, 23*(3/4), 5-22.

This article reports on a study of a telephone-delivered cognitive-behavioral group intervention for gay and bisexual men seeking help with maintaining safer sex habits. It focuses on the role of anonymous enrollment in helping to recruit participants who might not otherwise volunteer.

30. Rothblum, E. D. (1994). "I only read about myself on bathroom walls": The need for research on mental health of lesbians and gay men. *Journal of Consulting and Clinical Psychology, 62*, 213-220.

31. Sell, R. L. (1996). The Sell Assessment of Sexual Orientation: Background and scoring. *Journal of Gay, Lesbian, and Bisexual Identity, 1*, 295-310.

32. Silvestre, A. J. (1994). Brokering: A process for establishing long-term and stable links with gay male communities for research and public health education. *AIDS Education and Prevention, 6*, 65-73.

33. Tully, C. T. (1995). *Lesbian social services: Research issues.* New York: Harrington Park Press.

     This book examines a variety of issues impacting social work research on lesbians. Issues include research models, study design, ethical dilemmas, and a review of the research on lesbian health.

34. Walsh-Bowers, R. T., & Parlour, S. J. (1992). Researcher-participant relationships in journal reports on gay men and lesbian women. *Journal of Homosexuality, 23*(4), 93-112.

35. White, J. C. (1998). Challenges and opportunities in clinical research on lesbian health. *Journal of the Gay and Lesbian Medical Association, 2*(2), 55-57.

36. Woodman, N. J., Tully, C. T., & Barranti, C. C. (1995). Research in lesbian communities: Ethical dilemmas. *Journal of Gay & Lesbian Social Services, 3*(1), 57-66.

XII. Social Work Education Issues

1.   Akerlund, M., & Cheung, M. (2000). Teaching beyond the deficit model: Gay and lesbian issues among African Americans, Latinos, and Asian Americans. *Journal of Social Work Education, 36,* 279-292.

2.   Ben-Ari, A. T. (1998). An experimental attitude change: Social work students and homosexuality. *Journal of Homosexuality, 36*(2), 59-71.

3.   Berkman, C., & Zinberg, J. G. (1997). Homophobia and heterosexism in social workers. *Social Work, 42,* 319-331.

4.   Besner, H. F. & Spungin, C. J. (1998). *Training for professionals who work with gays and lesbians in educational and workplace setting*s. Washington, DC: Accelerated Development.

     This book provides many structured activities and other materials for use in educational/training workshops.

5.   Black, B., Oles, T. P., Cramer, E. P., & Bennett, C. K. (1999). Attitudes and behaviors of social work students toward lesbian and gay male clients: Can panel presentations make a difference? *Journal of Gay & Lesbian Social Services, 9*(4), 47-68.

6.   Black, B., Oles, T. P., & Moore, L. (1998). The relationship between attitudes: Homophobia and sexism among social work students. *Affilia, 13,* 166-189.

7.   Cain, R. (1996). Heterosexism and self-discloure in the social work classroom. *Journal of Social Work Education, 32,* 65-76.

8.   Cramer, E. P. (1997). Effects of an educational unit about lesbian identity development and disclosure in a social work methods course. *Journal of Social Work Education, 33,* 461-472.

9.   Cramer, E., Oles, T. P., & Black, B. M. (1997). Reducing social work students' homophobia: An evaluation of teaching strategies. *Arete, 21,* 36-49.

10. Gerdes, K. E., & Norman, J. (1998). Teaching social work students the breadth of gay and lesbian identity development. *Journal of Teaching in Social Work, 17,* 137-154.

11.   Green, R. J. (1996). Why ask, why tell? Reaching and learning about lesbians and gays in family therapy. *Family Process, 35,* 389-400.

12.   Mackelprang, R. W., Ray, J., & Hernandez-Peck, M. (1996). Social work education and sexual orientation: Faculty, student, and curriculum issues. *Journal of Gay & Lesbian Social Services, 5*(4), 17-31.

13.   Messinger, L., & Topal, M. (1997). "Are you married?": Two sexual-minority students' perspectives on field placements. *Affilia, 12,* 106-113.

14.   Morrow, D. F. (1996). Heterosexism: Hidden discrimination in social work education. *Journal of Gay & Lesbian Social Services, 5*(4), 1-16.

   This article suggests ways to minimize heterosexism in social work education, and it includes ideas for gay and lesbian content.

15.   Oles, T. P., Black, B. M., & Cramer, E. P. (1999). From attitude change to effective practice: Exploring the relationship. *Journal of Social Work Education, 35,* 87-100.

   This article reports on a study of the use of vignettes to improve students' anticipated professional behavior with gay and lesbian clients.

16.   Parr, R. G., & Jones, L. E. (1996). Should CSWE allow social work programs in religious institutions an exemption from the accreditation nondiscrimination standard related to sexual orientation? *Journal of Social Work Education, 32,* 297-313.

17.   Speziale, B. A. (1997). Introducing sexual diversity into social work education: A humanistic group approach. *Journal of Teaching in Social Work, 15,* 51-61.

18.   Thoresen, J. H. (1998). "Do we have to call it that?!" Planning, implementing, and teaching an LGBT course. In R. L. Sanlo (Ed.), *Working with lesbian, gay, bisexual, and transgender college students: A handbook for faculty and administrators* (pp. 255-263). Westport, CT: Greenwood Press.

   This chapter discusses several issues that might be confronted when developing a course on lgbt issues.

19.   Van Soest, D. (1996). The influence of competing ideologies about homosexuality on nondiscrimination policy: Implications for social work education. *Journal of Social Work Education, 32,* 53-64.

20.   Vasquez, M. J., & Eldridge, N. S. (1994). Bringing ethics alive: Training practitioners about gender, ethnicity, and sexual orientation issues. *Women & Therapy, 15*(1), 1-16.

Keyword Index

A note to the user: The following keyword index is intended to supplement the list of subject areas identified in the table of contents (TOC). It is not an exhaustive list of subject areas contained within the bibliography. The entries in the keyword index are found in other subject areas apart from their specific area categorized in the TOC. For example, when searching for literature on health care issues among lesbians, it is best to search the entries under the TOC subject area Health, then check the entries identified under health care issues in the keyword index for resources organized elsewhere in the bibliography.